BFI Film Classi

MW00532373

The BFI Film Classics is a series of books that introduces, interprets and celebrates landmarks of world cinema. Each volume offers an argument for the film's 'classic' status, together with discussion of its production and reception history, its place within a genre or national cinema, an account of its technical and aesthetic importance, and in many cases, the author's personal response to the film.

For a full list of titles available in the series, please visit our website: <www.palgrave.com/bfi>

'Magnificently concentrated examples of flowing freeform critical poetry.'
*Uncut*

'A formidable body of work collectively generating some fascinating insights into the evolution of cinema.'
*Times Higher Education Supplement*

'The series is a landmark in film criticism.'
*Quarterly Review of Film and Video*

'Possibly the most bountiful book series in the history of film criticism.'
Jonathan Rosenbaum, *Film Comment*

# The Shining

Roger Luckhurst

A BFI book published by Palgrave Macmillan

First published in 2013 by
**PALGRAVE MACMILLAN**

on behalf of the

**BRITISH FILM INSTITUTE**
21 Stephen Street, London W1T 1LN
www.bfi.org.uk

There's more to discover about film and television through the BFI. Our world-renowned archive, cinemas, festivals, films, publications and learning resources are here to inspire you.

Palgrave Macmillan in the UK is an imprint of Macmillan Publishers Limited, registered in England, company number 785998, of Houndmills, Basingstoke, Hampshire RG21 6XS. Palgrave Macmillan in the US is a division of St Martin's Press LLC, 175 Fifth Avenue, New York, NY 10010. Palgrave Macmillan is the global academic imprint of the above companies and has companies and representatives throughout the world. Palgrave® and Macmillan® are registered trademarks in the United States, the United Kingdom, Europe and other countries.

Front cover design: Mark Swan
Series text design: ketchup/SE14
Images from *The Shining*, © Warner Bros.; *The Legend of Hell House*, © Twentieth Century-Fox Film Corporation; *The Haunting*, © Metro-Goldwyn-Mayer, Inc/© Argyle Enterprises; *The Omen*, © Twentieth Century-Fox Film Corporation; *The Amityville Horror*, Cinema 77/Professional Films/American International Pictures; *The Evil Dead*, © Renaissance Pictures; *Friday the 13th*, Georgetown Productions; *The Fury*, Twentieth Century-Fox Film Corporation/Frank Yablans Presentations; *Scanners*, Filmplan International/Canadian Film Development Corporation; *Night of the Living Dead*, Image 10; *Psycho*,© Shamley Productions.

The excerpt from *Book VIII*, 'The Minotaur', *Ovid: Metamorphoses*, translated by A. D. Melville (1986), is reproduced with permission from Oxford University Press.

*Polymorphia*, page of manuscript © 2006 SCHOTT Music. Reproduced by permission. All rights reserved.

Set by Cambrian Typesetters, Camberley, Surrey
Printed in China

This book is printed on paper suitable for recycling and made from fully managed and sustained forest sources. Logging, pulping and manufacturing processes are expected to conform to the environmental regulations of the country of origin.

British Library Cataloguing-in-Publication Data
A catalogue record for this book is available from the British Library
A catalog record for this book is available from the Library of Congress

ISBN 978–1–84457–639–5

# Contents

Eagerly anticipated: a vast advertising budget was spent on hyping up *The Shining*

# 'The Shining'

## Introduction

*The Shining* opened in America on Memorial Day weekend 1980 after a saturation advertising campaign. The ominous and surreal trailer appeared in cinemas at Christmas 1979, a wall of blood cascading out of the lift shaft, rushing towards and swallowing the camera. Sickly yellow posters proliferated in newspapers and on billboards. From a closed set, where Kubrick had been cloistered on sound-stages for three years, the director promised 'the scariest horror film of all time'. For British audiences, unable to see *A Clockwork Orange* (1971) since Kubrick had withdrawn it over fears of copycat violence, the anticipation that this would be something even more transgressive was intense.

The film was released to derisive laughter. Pauline Kael, who had long accused Kubrick of valuing technical virtuosity over human story, suggested that the film was 'dumb', a Gothic story told without shadows or passionate emotion, and asked: 'Who wants to see evil in daylight, through a wide-angle lens?' 'We're not frightened,' she complained, 'because Kubrick's absorption in film technology distances us.' The London *Times* wondered how Kubrick had squandered five years since *Barry Lyndon* (1975) on such an expensive crock, a pulp horror pointlessly abstracted. It was, one *Sight & Sound* reviewer declared, 'an immensely trivial project'. *Variety* was baffled at the studied banality of the film, its airless imitation of terror that it could not communicate. The tone was off, the acting brash and grotesque. It would have taken a pro like John Carpenter – whose $320,000 *Halloween* (1978) was still turning phenomenal profits – a couple of months to knock off a shocker with a bit more energy and conviction.[1]

Brian de Palma, with a decade of disordered horror films behind him and the lurid sub-Hitchcock sexual thriller *Dressed to Kill* (1980) still in cinemas, launched a typically outspoken attack on auteurs who thought they could appropriate the lowly horror genre. 'They condescend to the genre, they don't understand it, they have no passion for it. And so they make terrible movies. I mean I was amazed by *The Shining*.'[2]

Stephen King, best-selling horror novelist and author of *The Shining*, the bruised writer of a screenplay Kubrick ignored, also hated the film. He conducted a press campaign against Kubrick's adaptation. 'You know what?' King asked. 'I think he wants to hurt people with this movie. I think that he really wants to make a movie that will hurt people.' In *Danse Macabre*, his 1981 critical reflections on horror, King called the film 'maddening, perverse and disappointing'.[3] Seventeen years later, evidently still smarting from Kubrick's rejection of his script and his imperious handling of the source novel, King scripted and produced a five-hour TV mini-series adaptation of his own to wrest the material back from Kubrick.

Kubrick in the Gold Room, with DP John Alcott

Typically, Kubrick did not respond in kind, but only as a film-maker. After the first weekend in New York, he sent out a team of editors to theatres to cut from prints of the film the epilogue, a scene in which the Overlook's manager, Ullmann, visits Wendy in hospital and tells her that her husband's body has not been found. The film would end, instead, on that photograph of Jack Torrance – a grand enigma for some viewers, an infuriating trick loop for others. Then, as *The Shining* was prepared for global release, Kubrick went in and cut the film down by another twenty-five minutes (the shorter, 119-minute version was the only one released in Britain until 2012, when the BFI issued the original American cut). The film did good business for Warner Bros., but Kubrick's tinkering did not rescue *The Shining* from another critical mauling from British reviewers.

Since the initial reaction, however, the reputation of the film has steadily grown to become one of the most admired horror films in cinema history. 'In some eerie fashion,' *The New York Times* noted in 1993, 'it gets better every year.'[4] Like the undead revenants of the Overlook, the viewer needs always to come back, to poke around in the corners of the frames and savour the charms of the corridor vistas. The jump-cuts, use of modernist music and subliminal inserts of Danny's visions of atrocity at the Overlook Hotel are regularly cited as some of the most effectively uncanny or frightening moments in cinema. They are embedded in western culture now, pastiched in TV shows like *Spaced* or *The Simpsons*.

Kubrick's relationship to the horror genre was soon grasped in a different way by more reflective critics. The director seemed to have a parodic or subversive approach, turning Gothic conventions on their head, locating the horror not in supernatural threats to the nuclear family but erupting from its domestic heart. Paul Mayersberg in *Sight & Sound* likened *The Shining* to a Henry James ghost story, mannered things from the fag end of the nineteenth century, tales that were oddly inconclusive. Rather like James's attitude to the Gothic, Mayersberg suggested, 'underlying many sequences in *The Shining* is a critique of the whole genre of horror movies'.[5] Kubrick's satirical subversions of noir, war film, science fiction or costume drama had a habit of being initially misread – as before, it would take the critics years to catch up with the genius of Kubrick the auteur.

Of course, the enigma of *The Shining*'s plotting, its odd ellipses and incompletions, the rich lore of its slippages and continuity errors, has by now generated an enormous body of commentary. There is a vast academic literature, shadowed, if not forthrightly subverted, by the extensive networks of conspiracy theory about the film that have found their natural habitat on the internet. Few films could sustain several documentaries dedicated to those readings, but *The Shining* is included in William Karel's *Dark Side of the Moon* (2002), Jay Weidner's *Kubrick's Odyssey: Secrets Hidden in the Films of Stanley Kubrick* (2011) and Rob Ager's *Kubrick's Gold Story* (uploaded to YouTube 2012). Rodney Ascher's *Room 237* (2012), a compendium of five obsessive readings, merely scratches the surface of theories that circulate about the occult purpose behind *The Shining*.

There are wacky theories: *The Shining* as coded apology by Kubrick for faking the film landing footage for NASA, say, with Danny's Apollo XI jumper the clincher. Or the Gold Room in the Overlook offers a concealed critique of Woodrow Wilson's foundation of the Federal Reserve. But it is sometimes hard to tell wacky theories apart from the 'respectable' close readings. Geoffrey Cocks has a near cabbalistic obsession with hidden numbers in *The Shining* – the multiples of 7, the recurrence of the number 42 on T-shirts, in the six trays of 7-Up, or the brief glimpse of the film *Summer of '42* on a TV. Divide 42 in half and you get to the summer of '21, the date of the masked ball, shown in an array of 7 x 3 photographs on the wall. This number theory derives from Cocks's university press monograph, *The Wolf at the Door: Stanley Kubrick, History and the Holocaust*. Cocks also argues that *The Shining* is a coded Holocaust text, this time stuffed with German typewriters and Nazi eagles, as well as being an exploration of American genocidal logic, marked out in carefully placed Calumet baking powder cans in the larder.

This is in the nature of paranoid readings: *The Shining* does to its viewers what the hotel does to its visitors – it makes them shine on things glimpsed that were perhaps never there, or were there all along, hiding in plain sight.

Here I am, another university professor, about to embark on yet another reading. Before I do, I have a confession to make. In 1980, at the age of thirteen, *The Shining* was a closed film to me. Before domestic video machines and the illicit trade in 'video nasties' that spurred a moral panic in 1984, it was not easy for young teenagers to see X-rated cinema, however much it appealed. Films like *Alien* (released in November 1979) existed for me in novelisations, movie tie-ins with colour-still inserts to dream over and try to animate. Horror was alluring because it existed in an economy of scarcity – it is impossible in an era of instant downloads to convey the frisson the simple letter 'X' on a film poster could have. Then, in the summer of 1980, BBC 2 ran their Saturday-night 'Horror Double Bill' series, an old classic coupled with a more titillating (and usually much worse) Hammer horror film from the 1970s. Partly, I think, because my parents were busy divorcing, an unusual and shameful thing in our middle-class suburb, I was given this odd Saturday-night licence to watch B-movies into the early hours. That series ruined a generation of boys for horror.

For *The Shining*, there was always the Stephen King novel (reissued with the movie poster as the cover), a book I read and reread with amazement at what now seem rather simple narrative possibilities of parallel plotting, the tricks of analepsis and prolepsis, the showy typographical representation of traumatic dissociation. King's book certainly had more psychological density than nasty shockers by James Herbert. I did not see Kubrick's *The Shining* until later, when it had acquired the patina of something strong enough that needed to be endured, a film that many a sensitive soul could not watch. By then it was a film for students, an art-house movie with an auteur's signature. Yet I have since spent my working life writing histories of telepathy, of trauma, of Gothic and science-fiction literature and film. The kernel of quite a lot of this work is found in the twisting corridors of *The Shining*. I, too, have been tempted to stay in the Overlook for ever and ever.

This book is not to be a fan's indulgence, however. I want to situate *The Shining* in a series of contexts that are not often brought to bear on a consideration of the film. I do not wish to treat the film in the formal isolation typical of auteur criticism. Instead, I want to look at the complex nature of horror cinema at the end of the 1970s and early 80s and think about the 70s horror revival in its general historical context as a moment of cultural crisis. In particular, I hope to open up the history of the tropes on which Kubrick's *The Shining* depends – the old dark house and the psychic child.

I also want to provide a diversity of approaches to the film itself, through a series of commentaries that follow the film in a roughly chronological way, allowing me to pick up on elements that are not restricted to one particular method or approach. The idea is not to offer a single, over-coherent interpretation (the fantasy of the paranoid reader), but rather an understanding of how the film is built as an open matrix that can support multiple avenues of possibility. We need to map the structure of the maze, rather than insisting there is only one route through it. The hope is that even readers who know the film extremely well will come away with some new resources for seeing it again in a fresh light.

## Swooping/tracking

The yellow VW Beetle struggles up the gradient of the mountain road on a startlingly calm and clear autumn day. The camera swoops over the car like a bird of prey toying with a hapless mouse. Or perhaps this is a bored or malicious angel, careening about the stratosphere looking for mischief, deciding whether or not to mess with this particular human story. Those old Greek gods always did make cruel, arbitrary interventions into human lives: there is no moral code in those vicious tragedies, only the wrong kind of attention from quixotic divines. The camera swings in close, right behind the Bug,

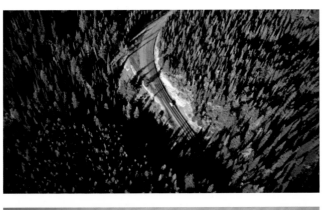

Demonic swoop #1, #2, #3

but then spins away over the edge of the road, careening down an abyss, perhaps uninterested after all in this tiny speck of life.

Yet the plangent opening chords on the soundtrack are already a warning: they echo the plainchant of the *Dies Irae*, the Wrath of God, used in the Requiem Mass for centuries. 'Day of Wrath, day that will dissolve the world in ashes.' The processed tones of this setting of the *Dies Irae* (Wendy Carlos based it on Berlioz's mocking use of the Latin hymn in the Witches' Sabbath section of the *Symphonie Fantastique*) begin to be worried by inhuman voices trilling something between delight and murder: 'The trumpet, scattering a wondrous sound/through the sepulchres of the regions/Will summon all before the throne.' Whoever is in that car has been marked to stand before the Judge: it is Death that is already in the air.

These opening sequences were shot in the Glacier National Park by a second unit of professional helicopter cameramen. Jeff Blythe recalls that they spent a month seeking the right conditions for those crystal-clear reflections of the lake, shooting blind from a very general brief, sending the dailies back to Kubrick in England. Another unit took the aerial photography of Timberline Lodge in Oregon, the hotel exterior used for the Overlook in the last of these opening shots.

This movement, the camera thrusting forward or back to devour space, to master it with absolute technical control, is Kubrick's signature gesture. The wide-angled, low tracking shot, focused on a single individual in relentless forward motion, had been there from *The Killing* (1956), where the apartments are linear successions of rooms, which allows the camera to track the anxious Sterling Hayden back and forth on the day of the heist without interruption. This was Kubrick's linear reduction of Max Ophuls's spatially roving camera and Orson Welles and Gregg Toland's use of deep focus in *Citizen Kane* (1941). Kubrick furthered the technique in dollies through the trenches in *Paths of Glory* (1957), the low and wide angle making the corridor of doomed men loom up around the focal point of General Mireau's unbearably smug face. In *A Clockwork Orange* and *Barry Lyndon*, Kubrick often reversed the direction, moving away from isolated faces in a stately reverse pull to reveal entrapment in spatial frameworks and systems no one individual could ever hope to control.

*The Shining* is remembered less for these helicopter shots, and more for the innovative use of Steadicam on the ground, where the camera's glide seems even more magical. Danny takes three decaying paths around the corridors of the Overlook in his pedal car: a simple circle through the Colorado Lounge and kitchen, an odd loop on the floor above, and a fragmentary turn through disjointed corridors higher up before he runs into the Grady girls. The wheels hammer across the wood floors and rumble over the rugs in a hypnotic rhythm (this was an accidental found effect of the set, not planned).

Kubrick pushed for technical innovation wherever he could. When he was shown footage of what the Steadicam could do by its inventors, releasing the camera from the tyranny of dolly tracks and handheld jitters, he asked immediately how low to the ground the rig could go. Garrett Brown, the inventor-operator of the Steadicam, which he had just used to film sequences for Sylvester Stallone's *Rocky* (1976), came over to advise Kubrick and ended up staying for most of the year of the *Shining* shoot.

The Steadicam rig displaces the weight through the body of the operator, leaving the camera floating free from knocks and jars, the cameraman's hands free to pan and tilt. Kubrick turned the device upside down, leaving the camera an inch above the ground. For the pedal-car loops, Garrett Brown sat in a wheelchair equipped with a speedometer so that it could be pushed at a steady pace for each take. There were no artificial walls, light-fills or lighting rigs inside the set, so as the Steadicam moved forward, the practical light fittings in the hotel corridors had to have their brightness dialled down by an operator as they came into view and up again as they passed behind the camera. Kubrick watched the takes through redesigned on-set monitors that better preserved the accuracy of his

framing. On the stairs that Wendy climbs near the climax of the film, Brown estimated that the repeated takes forced him to climb the equivalent of the Empire State Building carrying the rig. Worse was to come in the chase through the maze, Brown running backwards through artificial smoke and snow, the director demanding the camera remain a strict five inches above the floor. The wide-angle lenses would distort wildly beyond a very limited focal point, so Kubrick's already notoriously high rate of takes began to escalate in suffocating conditions.

Technical manipulation is the heart of *The Shining*'s enduring effect, but how it is achieved falls away in the dream-like, subjectless glide through the spaces of the hotel. The way in which the camera moves through these hallways introduced an extraordinary new emotion to cinema, evoking the kind of oneiric dread that the photographer Gregory Crewdson associates with anxiety dreams in

Garrett Brown, inventor of the Steadicam, with a pensive Kubrick in the Overlook maze

his photographic series about surburban America, *Hover* (1996). This is not the tired device of the subjective point of view of the camera-killer imported from Michael Powell's *Peeping Tom* (1960) or Carpenter's *Halloween*, then raking in the returns from its four-minute, single-take 'Panaglide' shock opening. Instead, it is something more stately and unnerving, an indifferent, complexly shifting gaze that explores the volumes of rooms and sometimes latches on to human figures within those spaces with vaguely malign intent. What looks is legion – and, we will shortly learn, telepathic. That demon hurtling around the mountain is back again.

This relentless horizontal glide of the camera also tells us a lot about the kind of adaptation Kubrick made of Stephen King's novel. King's book emphasises the vertical. The key revelations take place in the hotel basement, where the rickety boiler splutters and lies in wait for the explosive finale. As a Gothic model of the psyche, it is in the basement that Jack Torrance uncovers the history of the hotel, and recovers memories of the cycles of familial abuse that have damned him to uncanny repetition. A key early event happens to Jack on the roof. Danny will lure his father to the third floor, the highest place in the hotel, and furthest from the basement. The most overtly haunted place in the hotel is the lift, lurching into life at night, moving randomly up and down, decked with confetti from a party that has not quite yet fully re-materialised.

In contrast, Kubrick moves in an entirely lateral way, never using the lift but gliding in strict geometric lines through the lounge and foyer, pirouetting through the clutter of the kitchen or the kinks in the corridors. The camera swishes left to right along the edge of the Gold Room, there and back, a space it somehow fears to enter, knowing it to be impossibly too large to fit into the building it occupies, watching it bloom into undead life from the very edges. There are only two scenes set on stairs, the camera's diagonal glide cancelling out the jagged rise of the steps. The controlling metaphor of the film is not what is buried beneath, but what waits around the corner in the maze. Danny will survive the Overlook because he has traced out the escape routes over and over from the worm's-eye view, refusing to be seduced by the over-look, the gods that swoop from above. Jack is left looping in a cycle of eternal return, an empty spool circling on a flat deck.

No wonder King hated the film: doesn't it set about decisively and perversely to refuse the intrinsic architecture of Gothic horror, its sublime heights, deep shadows and dungeon depths?

## Overlook

When we look down at the Overlook Hotel from the helicopter, its roof peak evoking the Carpenter Gothic revival style, it is already ghosted by the American tradition of the old dark house, a haunted place that stretches back to the first settler Gothic fictions. The utopia of the American Republic was meant to escape from the ghosts of fallen Europe, but the Puritans only dragged these spectres with them, or conjured new ones out of the shadows.

H. P. Lovecraft imagined those fragile first settlements quivering amongst 'the vast and gloomy virgin forests in whose perpetual twilight all terrors might well lurk'. The Puritans demonised 'the hordes of coppery Indians whose strange, saturnine visages and violent customs hinted strongly at traces of infernal origins'.[6] The Overlook is a defiance of these primal forces. Ullmann, taking the new winter caretakers on a tour of the hotel, tells them that it was built on an old Indian burial ground and in the teeth of Indian attacks. Here is an echo of the foundational violence at the origin of the American Republic. Soon those early settlers were seized by fears of insidious possession from within the palisades rather than the imagined monsters beyond. The witch trials of the 1690s were hysterical attempts to purify communities already self-divided, already fallen back into the mess of history. The American Gothic is directly plugged into this panicky Puritan moment: Nathaniel Hawthorne, who wrote *The House of Seven Gables* (1851), was a direct descendant of witch-finder and hanging judge, William Hathorne.

Stephen King's *The Shining* owes direct debts to this tradition. The model for the Overlook is Shirley Jackson's 1959 novel *The Haunting of Hill House*, filmed with brilliant restraint as *The Haunting* by Robert Wise in 1963. Jackson premised her book on the idea that a psychic sensitive might create a dangerous amplifying effect on an already haunted house, the malignity curdling into something that can reach into the physical world with murderous intent. Eleanor, the vulnerable psychic of the team, feels herself disappearing 'inch by inch' into the house but wails at the prospect of her removal: 'I don't want to leave the house ever ever ever.' She gets her deathly wish: 'silence lay steadily against the wood and stone of Hill House, and whatever walked there, walked alone'.[7] Jackson based her story on the true investigation of Ballechin House in Scotland by the psychic sensitive Ada Goodrich-Freer for the Society for Psychical Research in 1897. Freer published claims about a persistent haunting that created a controversy over the methods and predisposed belief of psychical researchers. This is the realm of Henry James's *The Turn of the Screw*, another masterpiece of a manse filled with ghosts by the psychical pressures introduced by the governess, admirably filmed by Jack Clayton as *The Innocents* (1961).

Jackson's idea of psychic amplification influenced several important films in the early 1970s. Nigel Kneale's superbly creepy *The Stone Tape* (1972) was about scientists testing the theory that haunting is a kind of psychic recording that can be captured by new digital technology, leading to the death of the psychically sensitive woman on the team played by Jane Asher. John Hough's *The Legend of Hell House* (1973) had another group of psychic investigators, including a physicist and a young female medium, who encounter a more distinctly demonic haunting in an English mansion occupied by the spirit of a depraved occultist. Both of them die.

But baroque family secrets as much as occult forces are part of this tradition. In James Whale's *The Old Dark House* (1932), the hidden secret of the mansion is not the dying man at the first turn of the stair but the considerably madder brother hidden behind a locked door at the second turn. This tradition was still operating in the 1970s: in Dan Curtis's *Burnt Offerings* (1976), the ancient figure in the locked attic rooms dictates the uncanny repetitions that will snare a rather puzzled-looking Oliver Reed. Truly Gothic family relations drive the investigation of the labyrinths of domestic space in Tobe Hooper's *The Texas Chain Saw Massacre* (1974), an ancient grandad wheeled out to suck obscenely on the bloodied fingers of the last unlucky visitor to the house. In these films, plot is a progressive unveiling of domestic physical space that defies rational order and instead shows wrinkles and tears in the space–time continuum.

By the time *The Shining* appeared at the end of the decade, America had combined the domestic, psychical and occultist strands in another allegedly true haunting which gripped the popular imagination. *The Amityville Horror: A True Story* was a best-selling book in 1977 and the film version appeared in 1979, beginning a series about a malignant haunted house that shows no sign of ending (the documentary *My Amityville Horror* appeared in 2012). The hesitation between truth and fiction in the Amityville story (the first film is 'true', the sequel that provides a back-story, *Amityville II: The Possession* (1982), an avowed fiction) was surely part of the frisson. The possibility of the 'true' presence of hellish forces in a quiet domestic setting had driven the phenomenal success of *The Exorcist* (1974).

Perhaps this was one of the central problems of the early reception of *The Shining*. It must have seemed to be a compendium of narratives, plots and images that had been endlessly rehearsed through the horror boom of the 1970s. An isolated spooky house shot in distorting wide-lens panorama was the mode of every establishing shot of *The Legend of Hill House*. Menacing travelling shots through uncanny corridors pepper *The Haunting*. We had already seen a young child barrelling along corridors on a tricycle: this is how Damien topples his mother over the balcony in *The Omen* (1976). And George Lutz, the stepfather in *The Amityville Horror*, is a man who becomes possessed by the menacing spirits of the house, morphing physically into the previous owner who had murdered his family. He furiously sharpens his axe, muttering that 'these kids of yours need some goddamn discipline'. Shortly after *The Shining* appeared, *Amityville II* and *Poltergeist* (1982) would play on the suggestion of houses built on burial grounds to spectacular effect. *The Shining* bathes in borrowed tropes.

Genre offers the pleasure of recognition, a play of repetition, but also modulation and transformation. To understand the puzzlement with which *The Shining* was received in 1980, it is important to grasp the complex and variegated state of the horror film at the end of a decade of boom. So before the camera enters the hotel, following Jack Torrance into Ullmann's office, let's briefly consider Kubrick's odd place in the genre.

In many respects, *The Shining* fits into a sequence of major studio investment in horror, a mainstreaming of a low genre that is often traced to the success of Roman Polanski's *Rosemary's Baby* (1968) and particularly the phenomenal cultural impact of *The Exorcist*, a gross-out shocker backed by Warner Bros. that reaped several Oscar nominations. The model of investment was changing in the late 1970s, though. In a fascinating study, Richard Nowell has tracked how the independent production of *Halloween* was carefully designed to tempt mainstream distributors, cut to receive a safe 'R' rating and appeal to the widest demographic. It consequently became one of the most profitable films in cinema history. It created successive waves of 'slasher' cycles, which have had a huge influence on Hollywood. The *Nightmare on Elm Street* series, beginning in 1984, established New Line Cinema as a major studio, while the *Scream* series did the same for Miramax in the 1990s. When *The Shining* was released, it appeared in the midst of the first slasher cycle, fifteen films in fifteen months from January 1980. Unlike the brilliantly unsettling *Black Christmas* (1974), Bob Clark's overlooked original slasher to which *Halloween* was conceived as a sequel, the tone of the 1980s cycle was dominated by the punitive and

vicious logic of *Friday the 13th*, released alongside *The Shining* in May 1980. In October, British critics were reviewing *The Shining* next to *Terror Train*. It was Jamie Lee Curtis and a serial killer again, only this time on New Year's Eve. The tag line was 'Don't waste money on a return fare. You won't be coming back!'

But the 1970s horror boom was also marked by a counter-cultural move against the tasteful mainstreamed horror of *The Omen* and its copies. Lowly exploitation houses have always fuelled horror production (Jack Nicholson started his career in Roger Corman quickies like *The Cry Baby Killer* [1958] and *The Terror* [1963]), but a striking new kind of horror was emerging from places far

Déjà vu? *The Legend of Hell House* (1973), *The Haunting* (1963)

beyond this mode of industrial B-movie production. The key film in
this context was George A. Romero's *Night of the Living Dead*
(1968), with many of his local Pittsburgh investors appearing in the
film itself. Speaking explicitly to counter-cultural times in the
incendiary year of 1968, *Night*'s subversive repurposing of horror
and science-fiction elements managed something extraordinary:
a grisly, anti-authoritarian film that helped establish the 'midnight
cult movie', but which was also picked up by and shown at the
Museum of Modern Art in New York in 1970 as a piece of
revolutionary art. Romero would perform the same act of revision on
the vampire story in *Martin* (1976), a grungy post-industrial and

Déjà vu? *The Omen* (1976), *The Amityville Horror* (1979)

thoroughly secular take on the genre, before returning to the zombie in explicitly satirical mode in *Dawn of the Dead* (1978).

*Dawn* fostered its own late-1970s cycle of imitators, a delirious art-house mélange of the Italian *giallo* made famous by Dario Argento and the American undead. In 1980, in Italy, one might have endured Bruno Mattei's *Zombie Creeping Flesh* or Lucio Fulci's *City of the Living Dead*. Meanwhile, Romero's work in the 1970s was paralleled by a host of auteurs working beyond the bounds of the system: Larry Cohen, David Cronenberg, Tobe Hooper, Bob Clark, Wes Craven, and even Brian de Palma before his adaptation of Stephen King's *Carrie* (1976) catapulted him into the mainstream.

Taste and audience discrimination are very finely calibrated in this field. This kind of 1970s horror cinema has been described as 'art-horror', a hybrid of trash exploitation cinema with European art-house sensibility. It is a conspiracy of high and low cultural margins against the tyranny of the tasteful middlebrow, a bid for the disordered sublime against the merely beautiful. Horror fans tend to be extremely suspicious of anything that smacks of domestication or appropriation. So where would Kubrick fit?

It is telling that the geeky horror fan Stephen King trashed *The Shining*, but a short time later utterly embraced Sam Raimi's *The Evil Dead* when he first saw it at the Cannes film festival in 1982. King called it 'ferociously original' and claimed 'it worked because nobody in the organized film establishment would even *think* about trying it this way'.[8] It is striking to realise that whilst Kubrick's vast production machine was winding down on *The Shining* in 1979, Sam Raimi was spending twelve weeks in the backwoods filming what would become the most notorious video nasty of the lot. As Kubrick polished his lenses and ironed out bumps in the dolly tracking, Raimi was inventing the 'shaky cam' to send demons hurtling through the trees and spending months on stop-motion special effects of corpses decaying. Fans look for what Kim Newman calls 'trash vitality', the inventive energy that comes from improvising with limited resources. *The Shining* looks sedate and humourless in

comparison to *The Evil Dead*, out of sync with an era when 'horrality' (the mix of horror and hilarity) turned the special effects maestros into subcultural horror heroes for their operatic gross-out set pieces. *The Shining* was ubiquitous, pushed by a huge commercial advertising machine. In contrast, *The Texas Chain Saw Massacre* was completely unavailable (caught up in rights wrangles), and the world of Abel Ferrara's *Driller Killer* (1979) or *Ms. 45* (1981) was about to be banned in a moral panic typical of the new conservative cultural climate. This was cachet Kubrick could not match.

Yet *The Shining* can be read fruitfully through perhaps the most famous discussion of the horror film of this era. In *Hollywood from Vietnam to Reagan*, Robin Wood regarded the boom in horror in the 1970s as emblematic of a collapse of social repression and the conservative containments of classical Hollywood cinema. Wood positively welcomes the symptomatic incoherence and irresolution of New Hollywood during the decade. Inconclusive and enigmatic films like Penn's *Night Moves* (1975) or Scorsese's *Taxi*

*Driver* (1976) made cinema 'crack open before our eyes', their form directly reflecting that the 'dominant ideology' had '*almost* disintegrated' (that 'almost' is particularly lovely, full of hope). For Wood, the horror film was the most significant genre of the decade, because its abiding theme was 'the struggle for recognition of all that our civilisation represses and oppresses'. Wood was one of the first serious critics to claim that for all their apparent nihilism, *Night of the Living Dead* and *The Texas Chain Saw Massacre* had the real 'force of art'.[9]

Wood's schematic view was that the productive incoherence of 1970s cinema, where the subversive power of the unconscious erupted through the horror film, had been replaced in the 80s with a conservative counter-revolution in politics (the arrival of the New Right's Reagan and Thatcher) and a consequent backlash in cinema. Symptomatic was *Friday the 13th*, featuring a monster no longer from the id but representing the punitive superego that reinforces social norms and suppresses any dissident behaviour with extreme prejudice. Jason's mother successfully eliminates any burgeoning

The other release of May 1980: *Friday the 13th*

teenage sexual expression before horror SFX maestro Tom Savini slices her head off in glorious slo-mo.

The Shining lies symptomatically on the very cusp of these eras, the turn of the decade a moment, Wood suggests, of ideological hesitation. Kubrick's film is quintessentially inconclusive, enigmatic and open-ended. It is full of subversive commentary on the power of the patriarch, as so much horror of the 1970s seems to be. Yet it also appropriates the subcultural energies of the genre for a stately auteur cinema, funded from the deep pockets of Warner Bros. studios.

David Thomson similarly regarded The Shining as a cusp film. In his book Overexposures: The Crisis in American Filmmaking (1981), The Shining serves as a touchstone for Thomson's sense that 1980 is a critical year for American cinema. May 1980 was dominated not by Kubrick's long-awaited return, but by Friday the 13th and George Lucas's The Empire Strikes Back, heralding the box-office domination of movies for tweenies. Thomson's musings on The Shining conclude: 'As much as it is a parody of film, it is also a cry of despair over the medium.' It has the elevation of art, yet is also a 'weird folly' as a piece of mass entertainment.[10]

Typically, The Shining seems to slip between the categories of many of these schemas. It is at once high art and low culture, subversive yet utterly contained, an American studio film with European sensibility, and thus seemingly destined to please no one. For different audiences, Kubrick's film was too high or too low, fatally misread the conventions of the genre in its hauteur, or cunningly reinvented them in a way audiences and critics consistently missed.

The camera slow-fades from hovering with menace above the Overlook and descends to the human level. Jack enters Ullmann's office for the final interview. Ullmann was played with unctuous charm and a fine rug of hair by Barry Nelson, whose career reached back to the Hollywood noirs of the 1940s. Wisely, Kubrick ignored the homophobic tints in King's version of the hotel manager, his explicit dislike of the insider deal that landed Jack Torrance the job.

Whole back-stories are junked. In the foreground, the scene is there
for Ullmann to intone the story of the tragedy of the winter of 1970,
the murderous cabin fever suffered by Charles Grady, who killed his
lovely wife and daughters with an axe before stacking them neatly in
a guest room and then putting both barrels of a shotgun in his
mouth. Here is what the Fates dancing in the air above the hotel have
done, and have already decided to do again. But the scene is also
working its unsettling effect at a spatial level, too. That window
behind Ullmann's desk, the bright autumn light glaring through the
leaves? It is impossible: the floor plan of the Overlook can't have an
outside window there. How did the set designers overlook that, the
conspiracy theorists ask? It must *mean* something. But this is only the
first torsion of space that will confound the viewer inside the
Overlook. This Gothic labyrinth won't need darkness and shadow to
get you turned around, lost under bright lights in straight corridors.

## The psychic child

Meanwhile, down the mountain in Boulder, Jack's son Danny is
watching *Road Runner* cartoons at the kitchen table and his wife
Wendy is smoking and reading J. D. Salinger's iconic novel of

rebellious youth, *The Catcher in the Rye*. Their conversation is awkward and banal until Wendy seeks the opinion of Danny's imaginary friend Tony about spending the winter in the Overlook Hotel. Tony speaks to Mrs Torrance as a croaky alter ego through a bent finger: the classic sign of a child who is psychically split, alter personalities being the characteristic tactic of traumatic dissociation. In the mirror of the bathroom where Danny is doubled (the first of many such shots), Tony tells him his father already has the job and will ring through shortly with the news. The phone rings on cue. The child's spooky powers are confirmed in minor, domestic key. Jack is impatient with Wendy's forced joviality on the phone, talking over her. Tony then reveals to Danny the advent of the horrors to come in precognitive flashes of vision: the lift, the twins, his own future state of catatonic terror. The screen blacks out as the wave of blood crashes over us.

The precognitive and telepathic power of Danny Torrance is another generic marker that embeds *The Shining* in the horror boom around the time of release. Stephen King repeatedly turned to the notion that early trauma inflicted children and adolescents with a psychical wound that could bleed into supernatural powers.

Doubling mirrors

Carrie's rage at the familial and social repression of her sexuality finally erupts with catastrophic violence after a trail of minor displays of telekinetic ability from the start. The younger girl's pyrokinetic powers in *Firestarter* (filmed by Mark Lester with Drew Barrymore in 1984) prove equally apocalyptic, ending with a fire that consumes the government facility and the manipulative substitute father trying to harness her psychical skills. Yet King tapped a generic association of extrasensory powers with persecuted children, popular in science-fiction stories at least since John Wyndham's *The Chrysalids* (1955) or A. E. van Vogt's *Slans* (1940).

The 1970s and early 80s was a cultural high point for these uncanny, psychic children or marginalised adults in cinema. In de Palma's *The Fury* (1978) or Cronenberg's *Scanners* (1981), these maligned yet valuable 'freaks' can cause their enemies to explode spectacularly in extraordinary set pieces. In *The Sender* (1982), a traumatised and amnesiac young man is able to project telepathic dreams onto those around him, a disturbing projective ability explored in coma patients in the Australian film *Patrick* (1978) and even more apocalyptically in *The Medusa Touch* (1978), in which Richard Burton pulls down a cathedral on the heads of its clueless congregation from his sickbed. Perhaps, too, *The Shining* evokes memories of the imaginary yet murderous older brother in Robert Mulligan's curiously unresolved film about a boy killer, *The Other* (1972). Even in the relatively tame *Poltergeist*, it is the girl who is the conduit for the haunting, because she has greater sensitivity to the invisible powers that seep through the TV signals and electrical wirings of the house.

Yet the cute Carol Anne is a twee Spielberg figure: just as often, kids in 1970s horror films are demonic forces, catastrophic disruptive presences, advents of disaster. The Gothic is often about little else than male terrors of female reproduction and the arrival of the monstrous infant. Rosemary's baby, who has her father's eyes, is followed by the chaos of hideous births in *It's Alive* (1974) or *The Brood* (1979), or the wildly incoherent life cycle of the creature

in *Alien*, a primal nightmare of male birthing. In *Don't Look Now* (1973), traumatic grief produces psychic flashes in the father. But these are not of the lost child, only a hideous crone who will be the agent of the father's death. Donald Sutherland mistakes portents for flashbacks. In a more avowedly religious framework, Regan is occupied by the demon Pazuzu in *The Exorcist*, and Damien ups the stakes as the

Summoning telepathic powers in *The Fury* (1978) and in *Scanners* (1980)

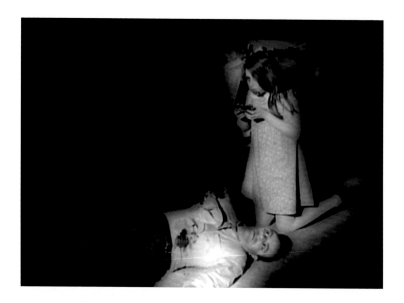

returning Antichrist in *The Omen*. The parents, the baby-boomer generation now arriving at parenthood themselves, are seemingly powerless, stricken with terror, before this appalling progeny. In the basement in *Night of the Living Dead*, the daughter Karen munches on her father's arm, looks up and then advances inexorably on her mother, who waits, passive and paralysed with fear, before being stabbed to death with a garden trowel.

What is going on? So much 1970s horror is set in a domestic space where the child is the ambivalent figure, an apparently innocent victim who can flip into demonic destroyer in the blink of an eye. William Paul has rather provokingly suggested that there is a trail of post-war American films starting with *The Bad Seed* in 1956 (about the eight-year-old murderous little girl Rhoda) in which the plot allows its adult audiences to indulge in fantasies of punishing children. One of the controversies surrounding *The Exorcist* was the mental and physical tortures the child actor Linda Blair had to endure on set. Despite the ostensible plot to rid a child of demonic

Karen, munching on her dad, in *Night of the Living Dead* (1968)

possession and return her to innocence, Paul suggests that the film 'makes a powerful case for the value of child abuse'.[11] Aren't many key horror films of the era about the crisis induced amongst children by the absence of paternal authority – Regan's vanished father, the entirely absent parents and ineffectual authorities of *Halloween*, the usurped paternity of Robert Thorn in *The Omen*?

In the 1970s, the divorce rate in America peaked, and a conservative backlash in defence of the family was wracked with anxiety over teenage pregnancy, youth crime, inner-city violence and 'stranger abductions' (following the kidnap of six-year-old Etan Patz in Manhattan in May 1979 and the huge media circus that surrounded this disappearance). Panics about sexual abuse of children began to surface as a result of feminist activism in the late 1970s: Florence Rush's *The Best Kept Secret: Sexual Abuse of Children* appeared in 1980.

Conservatives blamed permissive parenting: the child-centred world of Benjamin Spock's self-help manuals had produced a generation of privileged brats resenting any discipline or authority. Children could even be feared by family values campaigners. In 1970, Richard Nixon's psychotherapist, Dr Arnold Hutschnecker, gained notoriety for writing a memo to the president that allegedly proposed that all seven- and eight-year-olds should be tested for violent and homicidal tendencies. Even without this panic narrative, the medicalisation of child behaviour problems accelerated in the 1970s. Ritalin became a popular drug to manage 'attention deficit' in children. The kids were revolting.

*The Shining* is shot through with these debates and anxieties. As we shall see, the film is an overt meditation on the family romance, another of Kubrick's satires on patriarchal authority, this time rewriting Freud's already fairly Gothic Oedipal struggle in grand, histrionic terms. Danny Torrance is another 1970s psychic child whose magical thinking allows him to evade the marshalled forces of a punitive and psychotic patriarchal order. In this sense, he is entirely a product of the genre and his times.

Yet it is also the case that Kubrick offers a rather different emphasis from many of the films that surrounded the release of *The Shining*. The psychic fantasy explored by horror cinema about telepathic powers is nearly always about heightened agency: the ability actively to project ideas, to 'push' the weak wills of others; even, at the most extreme, to kill enemies by the power of thought alone. This is 'the fury' or the rare power of 'scanners'. The shining, in contrast, is hardly an active talent at all, but is about the involuntary receipt of terrifying scenes, fugitive and incomprehensible flashes that the boy can barely remember when he returns to consciousness. For the latter half of the film, the shining causes Danny such trauma that he dissociates into a trance state: 'Danny isn't here, Mrs Torrance,' Tony croaks from the empty shell of the boy's body. The boy Danny will only return to himself, significantly enough, as he escapes his father in the maze.

*The Shining* does not explore telepathy as the willed singular consciousness, but rather how it might disperse and multiply consciousness. In rigorously exploring this idea in both the content and form of *The Shining*, Kubrick is actually much closer to the earnest Victorian investigators who coined the term telepathy in 1882, rather than sharing the fantasies of modern popular culture. *Tele + pathos*, a paradoxical 'distant feeling', was the name given by poet and psychologist Frederic Myers to the 'communication outside the recognised channels of sense' that was pursued by the Society for Psychical Research. For the SPR, this was not a talent that could be acquired and trained but instead a rare openness to the psychic flashes of the thoughts of others that could not be controlled. Sensitive receivers were likely to be in odd receptive states of trance or in the twilight between sleep and waking; women and children could be more sensitive than men.

The Society collected anecdotal evidence of 'spontaneous' cases of telepathic communication, ordering them into wonderfully evocative categories in earnest reports that filled hundreds of pages. They believed that many instances of telepathic communication were associated with extreme emotional states, moments of intensity, terror or death, which would produce what they called a 'telepathic phantasm', a hallucinatory image that was nevertheless a real trace of psychic disturbance. The phantasm was a psychic distress signal that would be thrown out, often to loved ones, regardless of physical distance, across the globe. This is how Danny signals to Dick Hallorann from Colorado to Miami.

The SPR also renamed the haunted house a 'phantasmogenetic centre', a place where a psychical remainder from the past 'modifies a certain portion of space, not materially or optically, but in such a manner that specially susceptible persons may perceive it'.[12]

Ghosts became 'exuviae of past thoughts and emotions' and the psychically sensitive experienced time distortions, which meant that they picked up not only traces of the past but also of the future.[13] These premonitions were also tagged in a taxonomy of psychical phenomena they termed not super-natural but merely super-normal – facts of nature, yet awaiting scientific explanation. In his interview with Michel Ciment on *The Shining*, Kubrick said of ESP that 'we are just short of conclusive proof of its existence'. This is the classic language of psychical researchers: scientific proof has always been just around the corner for 130 years now.[14]

In Danny, Kubrick brings together both a cinematic history of the psychical child and an occult history of psychology. He creates in Danny a figure who registers receptive vulnerability to the traumas embedded in his environment, but also conveys the anxiety that children might be vehicles for other psychic occupants, conduits for strange and inexplicable forces.

### The missing doctor

The actor Anne Jackson gave a long account to Kubrick's biographer Vincent LoBrutto of her anxious dealings with Kubrick on set regarding her role as the doctor who visits Danny after his first seizure and visions in the bathroom. She was given no context, no

back-story about the character, no clarification on whether the
doctor was a clueless GP or an expert paediatrician. And there was
no direction on set, other than the massive accumulation of takes
and Kubrick's insistent, blank command from behind his monitors:
'Let's go again.'

There is a structural elegance to the double interviews that open
*The Shining*. Jack Torrance is suppressing something, a coiled rage,
in the polite responses he gives to Ullmann in his office; the enigmatic
Bill Watson looks continually askance at him as if his vacuous
questions and responses fool no one. In parallel, the doctor checks
Danny over and then settles down amongst flung copies of the *New
York Review of Books* to interview the skittish Mrs Torrance.

In the version released outside America, however, the doctor
vanishes entirely, snipped from the frame in Kubrick's re-edit, which
narrows *The Shining* down relentlessly to the primal family romance.
It turns the name Anne Jackson in the opening credits into another
vanished ghost of the Overlook which only those with the shining
can see. The conversation with the doctor adds weight to the family
dynamics, establishing Jack's history of alcoholism and his moment
of violence towards Danny five months earlier. Drunk, late, not in the

Anne Jackson, the 'missing' doctor

best of moods, Jack pulls Danny away from his scattered papers but in doing so dislocates the boy's shoulder. We thus get to hear another version of this story before Jack's self-piteous confession to the barman Lloyd later in the film. This account is told in awkward, ashamed tones by Wendy, a justificatory story of a cowed wife, spoken under the blank gaze of the doctor. You can see the medic, motionless, shocked, doing the silent calculations about the appearance of Danny's imaginary friend Tony and the act of violence, the dissociation from parental abuse Tony likely represents.

Left in, the scene places *The Shining* on the cusp of a particular model of familial trauma and abuse that would become dominant in American culture in the 1980s. It makes more sense of the sullen and suppressed self that Jack is struggling to maintain with his family and the world: he has been forced to be on his best behaviour. With the scene edited out, the film becomes more enigmatic. It decisively shifts focus away from the psychology of Danny (or the role of Wendy) towards Jack's struggle with his paternal authority over the incomprehensible beings of wife and child. Without this domestic back-story played out in Vermont, the film becomes a more abstract and mythic grid of possibility. These elements – the local and the mythic – constantly struggle in the final edit.

Kubrick was fond of quoting the 1929 book *Film Technique* by the Russian film-maker and theorist Vsevolod Pudovkin: 'The foundation of film art is *editing* ... The film is not *shot*, but *built*, built up from the separate strips of celluloid that are its raw material.' Things recorded by the camera, Pudovkin said, were only so many 'dead objects': 'The man photographed is only raw material for the future composition of his image in the film, arranged in editing.'[15] Kubrick enjoyed editing more than any other process of film-making, and he must have been acutely aware how the different edits of *The Shining* in effect created a different narrative arc, a different architecture to the film. I watched the version without the doctor's visit for years, unaware that there was another scene that doubled Jack's interview in Ullmann's office. The scene's absence

doesn't make it a worse film, only one with a different shape and a
more enigmatic, mythical tone.

Actually, what Kubrick chose to cut from the shooting script is
unusually visible in both released versions of the film. In the novel,
Jack Torrance finds (or is directed to find) a large book of cuttings in
the basement that details the perverse and murderous history of the
Overlook Hotel, the years of failed openings and revamps, the
deaths and suicides, before a shady gangland figure takes over in
1945 and an execution occurs in the Presidential Suite. The place has
barely made money since its re-launch in the 1960s, and the Grady
murders had been a serious threat to the fragile recovery of its
reputation as a resort hotel. This is the cuttings book that will
inspire Jack Torrance to abandon the terrible play he had hoped to
finish during the winter and instead begin to write a history of the
hotel. Jack baits Ullmann on the phone with the hidden scandals of
the hotel that he is about to expose.

None of this narrative survives in the film, except that the book
of cuttings does in fact appear on Jack's writing desk next to his
typewriter about halfway through, and stays there in plain sight.
The prop is a lovingly created document, filled with newspaper

The mysterious book of cuttings, foreground

stories about the Great War, American murders, crimes and misdemeanours. It lies open in some scenes, and Jack is clearly dipping into it for source material. There were seemingly elaborate plans for the messages these cuttings might convey to Jack, but this material did not pass the cut, the film that Kubrick built in the editing room. It means that there is no explanation for Jack's transition from terrible writer's block ('lots of ideas: no good ones'), his distracted hurling of a ball at the walls of the Colorado Lounge, to the suddenly furious concentration and hours of typing.

The reveal for the unhinged manuscript he is working up is one of the finest moments of the film, made possible by clearing out the clutter of King's back-story. Yet unusually, perhaps, *The Shining* leaves a trail of the editing choices Kubrick made, and the two versions, with the doctor and without, amplify this opportunity to study his decisions.

### The family romance

The yellow VW Beetle struggles up the gradient of the mountain road. This time, after an aerial echo of the opening, we are allowed inside the car: the family is together for the first time. The back projection reminds you of Hitchcock: the twisting roads in *Vertigo* (1958) or Marion's anxious journey that leads her fatefully to the Bates Motel. In this scene, we already know that Jack is nuts: there is an aggression in his responses, a flare of anger in the eyebrows, and sadism as he licks his lips over the story of the Donner Party. Wendy tries to stop Jack telling the tale. 'Don't worry, Mom, I know all about cannibalism. I saw it on TV,' Danny says. 'See,' Jack seethes with rage and contempt, 'it's okay, he saw it on the television.'

In keeping with 1970s paranoia about family collapse, this was the era of the 'anti-psychiatry' movement, when figures like R. D. Laing argued that the normal behaviours defined by society were driving western families insane. Laing's ally David Cooper wrote in *The Death of the Family* that the 'bourgeois family unit' was a 'suicide pact' which generated only rage, alienation and

inauthentic living: it demanded 'sacrificial offering' and 'passive submission to invasion by others'.[16] Jack already seems to agree, seething in these appalling constraints. *Kramer vs. Kramer* it ain't; instead, it's as if Nicholson's character in *Five Easy Pieces* (1970), Robert Dupea, has been caught by the awful restrictions of bourgeois family life after all.

The gruesome tale of the 1846 pioneers caught by snow in the Sierra Nevadas, leading to contested claims that they ate their dead to survive, also feeds directly into the most Gothic Oedipal fantasies Sigmund Freud claimed that he had found in his neurotic patients. In an essay called 'Family Romances', Freud argued that fantasies about the loss or death of parents was part of a necessary process of separation. 'A boy is far more inclined to feel hostile impulses towards his father than towards his mother,' he explained, before exploring fantastical scenes of punishment and beating in young children, and nightmares of being devoured. He asked readers not to 'turn away in horror from this depravity of the childish heart': these exaggerated fantasies, after all, were the basis of many myths and fairy tales, functional stories that tell children how to come into being as autonomous individuals.[17]

The Torrance nuclear family

Kubrick certainly read Freud as part of his preparation for *The Shining*. Diane Johnson, his co-screenwriter, was picked not just for her novels of urban paranoia, such as *The Shadow Knows* (1974), but also because she was an English professor who taught a course on the Gothic. Together, for the purposes of research, they read Freud's famous essay 'The Uncanny', which describes how the homely can harbour the strangely unhomely, become a place of terror and alienation rather than security and identity. (Remember that Jack Torrance will describe the family living quarters in the Overlook as 'homey' in front of the door on which Danny will scrawl REDRUM.) Freud's essay was published in 1919, the year, incidentally, that was scripted to be the date on the caption in the photograph at the end of the film. In 'The Uncanny', fathers are devouring and punitive, untrustworthy and castrating, driving their sons mad, just as they do in Freud's take on the story of Oedipus Rex.

Kubrick readjusted the emphasis of this Oedipal structure away from the psychology of the son to focus on the father. It is the father's Oedipal rages that drive Kubrick's tale, his wounded paternal authority. Freud sometimes told this family romance in ironic mode; on other occasions in case studies that skirted close to true psychotic terror. He pushed the primal relation of father to son to Gothic levels in his case history of 'The Wolf Man', where the key traumatic memory behind all the neurotic behaviours of his disturbed patient is a sexual scene between the parents that the Wolf Man had witnessed as a young child. He can only imagine the sex act as a violent, cannibalistic attack on his mother, taken, Freud coyly states, *'more ferarum'* (from behind), the Latin meaning 'in the manner of wild beasts'.[18] The father's animal desire is fused with the boy's terror of images of wolves from fairy-tale illustrations of 'Little Red Riding Hood' and the 'The Wolf and the Seven Little Goats': in both tales, the wolf eats up all those who cannot match his cunning. This hidden scene drives terrible phobias and a recurring nightmare of wolves waiting for him in the trees outside his bedroom.

There is a wolf waiting in the sadistic grin of Jack Nicholson in this scene in the car. It anticipates the explicit arrival of the Big Bad Wolf at the emotional climax of the film, swinging the axe whilst he intones lines from the 'Three Little Pigs'. Fourteen years later, of course, Nicholson finally got to play a werewolf in Mike Nichols's film *Wolf*, disappointingly literalising everything that lurked so unstated in this scene.

## The Colorado Lounge

'Closing Day': Jack chucks away the copy of *Playgirl* he is so casually reading in the lobby, and meets Ullmann. I always laugh at the sheer volume of luggage the family have brought with them (how did it fit in that Beetle?) and the fury of Bill Watson's 'Fine!' as he is told to move this vast pile of suitcases up to the Torrance's new quarters. It is his only line in these scenes. Ullmann leads Jack and Wendy on a tour of the hotel, Watson trailing sullenly behind. Danny throws darts in the Games Room.

The only time the characters use the lifts is when we see Mr Ullmann holding open the lift doors for the Torrances. He takes them on their first traversal of the Colorado Lounge, a set clearly based on the famous Ahwahnee Hotel in Yosemite National Park, a remote luxury hotel built at huge expense in the 1920s. This is a bravura tracking shot moving past windows that were so brightly lit by lighting rigs emitting up to a million candlepower that the temperature on set was uncomfortably high. We wince on Jack's behalf at Wendy's gauche reactions to the height of the windows, the light, the Navajo designs on the walls: 'My God, this place is fantastic, isn't it hon? ... As a matter of fact, this is probably the most gorgeous hotel I've ever seen.' Shelley Duvall's eccentric delivery, plucked out of her usual Robert Altman ensemble-playing and cruelly isolated, is pitch-perfectly awkward. Large arrays of photographs cover the walls, creep around corners and up stairwells. Kubrick selected these from the Warner Bros. archive, mainly from the 1920s, saturating the room in Hollywood history.

Significantly, this is where Ullmann sketches in some of the Overlook's back-story.

Kubrick was always the master of mapping architectural space. The right-to-left sweep of the camera dwarfs the actors in a huge volume of space, keeping them in deep background. These are the kind of sets that doom the human figures in *Dr Strangelove* (1964) and *2001* (1968) to be minor cogs in vast, deathly machineries that they will never control. The camera passes in front of the stairwell where violence between the couple will finally erupt, meeting them as they pass behind it, just as Ullmann is claiming for the hotel the jet set, four presidents and 'all the best people'.

In fact, they stop next to a prominent image on the wall of a Native American tribal chieftain. We are invited to read the cues in the room historically, and clearly in relation to the violent history of the American frontier and the destruction of the Native Americans. The Overlook was built between 1907 and 1909, Ullmann explains in another tracking shot along the exterior of the hotel, 'and I believe they actually had to repel a few Indian attacks as they were building it'. (The Ahwahnee Hotel was built on the site of an indigenous Miwok village, rudely incorporating the designs of the culture it effaced.) That vanished culture persists in the Diné/Navajo designs in the wall-hangings and reproduced sand-paintings, in the marble floors and ceiling details, and on the Calumet cans in the storeroom and Wendy's yellow jacket as she talks on the CB radio.

This is the prompt to read *The Shining* in the tradition of the American Gothic. What haunts America is a violent history – the settlers who systematically murdered the Native Americans, built wealth on the backs of African slaves, and suffered the parricidal guilt of a rebellious colony that shook off the colonial father to become an independent republic in the War of Independence. The critic Leslie Fiedler memorably called the 'cheap jack machinery' of the Gothic a dominant strand in American culture because it remained 'a pathological symptom rather than a proper literary movement'.[19] We could say the same of the persistence of horror in

American cinema. The terror of the wilderness and the Lovecraftian monsters said to populate it has never gone away.

Is the space of the Colorado Lounge meant to evoke the unspoken atrocity that lies beneath the settler nation, the bond of blood that underpins the white fraternity of national manhood? Geoffrey Cocks suggests that the apparently unmotivated image of blood welling from the lift shaft is 'the blood of centuries, the blood

Kubrick's tracking of space in the Colorado Lounge

of millions, and, in particular, the blood of war and genocide in
Kubrick's own country'.[20] Yet Cocks sets off on the trail of coded
references to the Jewish Holocaust, rather than pursuing American
history. Fredric Jameson argues that Kubrick's evocation of a hotel
stuck hauntingly in the 1920s is about a nostalgia for the wealth and
confidence in rigid racial and class hierarchies of the pre-war era.
This is a little vague, too: I wonder if Kubrick was specifically aware

of the growing Native American activism of the 1970s, such as the
occupation of Alcatraz (between 1969 and 1971) and the site of the
Wounded Knee massacre (in 1973) by the American Indian
Movement, Red Power and other activist groups. These occupations
forced attention on the question of land rights and forgotten
genocidal histories in America. If there is a deliberate semiotic echo
of these events in *The Shining*, Kubrick does it obliquely, in the deep
space of the design, rather than exploiting the melodrama of undead
vengeance of Native spirits used by Stephen King in *Pet Sematary*
(1983) or by Tobe Hooper in *Poltergeist*.

The tour of the Colorado Lounge and the Overlook also,
in a way, traverses cinema history. Although the image is crisp, the
light is blinding and there are no shadows, we are in the American
haunted house, the halls echoing with the immediate influences of
*The Amityville Horror* and *Burnt Offerings*, but working back
through time to echo the clamouring ghost of *The Haunting*, or the
motel stuffed with dead birds overlooked by the widow's peak of the
mother's house in *Psycho* (1960), then further back to Kane's cursed
mansion, Xanadu, or the ruin of Norma Desmond's baroque pile in
*Sunset Blvd.* (1950), or James Whale's *The Old Dark House*, a film
in which the main set is dominated by an ominous staircase.
The theory of ghosts in *The Shining* may be borrowed from psychical
research, but it is the fate of Kubrick the cineaste to be haunted by
movie history, each frame a palimpsest overpainted by a thousand
vanished films.

## What's up, Doc?

Spliced into the hotel tour is Danny's close encounter with the
Grady daughters, those unnerving phantasms. They echo, of course,
Diane Arbus's famous photograph of twins, taken in 1967, which
brilliantly catches the cultural taboo, the unsettling weirdness of
doubled, identical selves (in many cultures, twins have been regarded
as supernatural portents and killed at birth). They stand in the
double doorway of the Games Room, shadowed by a ski poster

that some see as containing a menacing figure of a minotaur.
Their appearance is accompanied by a high-pitched tinnitus sound
that in the next few scenes will become associated with moments of
access to telepathic vision.

These conspiratorial twins are very solid – they are reflected in
the floor as they turn, smirk, communicate something silently (as we
think all twins do) and walk away, even though their shiny shoes
make no sound. They don't seem to be of quite the same order as the
psychic flashes shown to Danny by his own psychic twin, Tony.
Yet minutes later he will say nothing of them to Dick Hallorann,
as if he cannot remember the encounter. Danny has been found
wandering the hotel by Ullmann's secretary, perhaps already
dissociated: the girls wish to enchant him, to lure him in, after all.
The enigma of the twins drives much conspiracy theory: if they *are*
twins, for instance, then can they really be Grady's daughters, who
Ullmann states were eight and ten years old? Might they not signify
something else, subliminally encoded? Of course! All ghosts are signs
of broken story, demanding someone takes up their narrative,
in whatever spirit, and bear witness to silent wrongs.

Wendy shines a bit: all mothers shine a little around their kids,
the cook Dick Hallorann observes in King's novel. She catches

The Grady sisters stop by

Hallorann out when they exit the freezer as he escorts Wendy and
Danny on a tour of the vast kitchen: 'Mr Hallorann, how did you
know we called him Doc? We call him Doc sometimes, you know,
like in the Bugs Bunny cartoons, but how did you know that?'
She's insistent she hasn't used the nickname. He brushes off his little
psychic slip by bending down to Danny and offering a feeble
impersonation: 'What's up, Doc?' In the storeroom, he will shine on
Danny in one of only two instances of active telepathic
communication in the film, accompanied by the same high-pitched
tinnitus tone: 'How d'you like some ice cream, Doc?' Over ice cream,
the cook will gloss what it means to shine.

Many fragments of popular culture are referenced throughout
*The Shining*, from the *Road Runner* cartoons playing off screen in
Boulder, and again in the family quarters of the Overlook, or the
cartoons on the TV in Durkin's car hire, to the Seven Dwarfs stuck
on Danny's bedroom door, his Mickey Mouse jumper or the *Summer
of '42* that he watches on TV with his mother. Later, Jack and Danny
will play Tom and Jerry amongst the clattering frying pans of the
kitchen and in the deadly circuits of the maze. Hallorann does not
have to reach deep into the mind of Danny to pull out the Bugs
Bunny catchphrase.

'What's up, Doc?'

References to these brash, epic conflicts, the Looney Tunes that premiered in the 1940s, accumulate alongside very deliberate echoes of fairy tales, whose plots the cartoons so often rehashed. The Grimm brothers' version of 'Hansel and Gretel' is referenced in the kitchen scene. Wendy, overwhelmed by the size of the place (as the Steadicam weaves backwards through the tables and equipment), tells Dick: 'This whole place is such an enormous maze, I feel I'll have to leave a trail of breadcrumbs every time I come in.' Perhaps she should have recalled that in the Grimm tale, the breadcrumbs are eaten by the birds in the forest, which means that the abandoned children cannot find their way home and get imprisoned in the gingerbread house. (In fact, Shelley Duvall was already an avid collector of fairy-tale books and started producing the TV show *Fairy Tale Theater* in 1982.)

Just as the witch wants to fatten the children up to devour them, Jack will turn into the Big Bad Wolf from the 'Three Little Pigs', and Danny must learn something from the third little pig and from Little Red Riding Hood – at least in some versions of her fate – about outwitting the wolf that hides in human clothing. There are also echoes of the folk tale collected by Charles Perrault called 'Hop o' My Thumb', in which the smallest boy, the runt of the family, defeats a menacing ogre.

Danny is punished because he plays out the plot of Perrault's 'Bluebeard' in relation to the lure of Room 237. Hallorann says: 'There ain't nothing in Room 237, but you ain't got no business going in there anyway, so stay out!' Bluebeard's new wife manages for a while to keep away from the forbidden room, but finally steals the key, opens the door and sees the severed heads of his previous wives reflected in a pool of blood. She drops the key and cannot remove the bloodstain, the detail that betrays her transgression. There is murder at the heart of every marriage.

As early as 1971, Kubrick had said in interview: 'I've always liked fairy tales and myths, magical stories. I think they are somehow closer to the sense of reality one feels today than the equally stylized "realistic" story.'[21]

At yet another level, *The Shining* invokes the structure of Greek myth, from the tragedy of Oedipus to the brave Theseus, who enters the Cretan labyrinth and slays the minotaur to whom maidens are sacrificed annually. He escapes by retracing the thread given to him by Ariadne, defying the trap built by Daedalus, that 'mazy multitude of winding ways', as Ovid puts it in *The Metamorphosis*. There is a reason we see Wendy leading Danny through the maze in those early autumn days: she is his thread out.

These layers of legendary and folkloric tales, stubs of story scattered through *The Shining*, make the plot resonate beyond the local level, reinforcing the sense of dread, because this hapless trio are merely repeating trajectories that have been told and retold for millennia. At the same time, though, they reinforce Kubrick's particular contribution to how the 1970s horror film exposes the hidden madness of the nuclear family. Kubrick and Diane Johnson were heavily influenced by their reading of the psychoanalyst Bruno Bettelheim, whose study *The Uses of Enchantment: The Meaning and Importance of Fairy Tales* had appeared in 1975. For Bettelheim, the fairy tale addressed the 'chaotic, angry, and even violent fantasies' of children and helped civilise their unconscious desires. The 'Hansel and Gretel' story concerns separation, fear of abandonment and the growth of autonomy. At the primal core of the story, the children's primitive oral gratifications (setting about eating the gingerbread house) get them into trouble, and they are only rewarded through behaving in a socialised way, acting according to reality rather than pure pleasure. The 'Three Little Pigs' presents a wolf that stands 'for all asocial, unconscious, devouring powers against which one must learn to defend oneself', whilst 'Bluebeard' has less an educative function than merely confirming the child's idea 'that adults have terrible sexual secrets'.[22]

*The Uses of Enchantment* was influential at the time, but I also wonder if Bettelheim's earlier study *The Empty Fortress* lurks as an influence on *The Shining*, a work that suggests that autism or psychosis in childhood are products of parental conflict and the inability to love children. Danny's traumatised vacancy and his wild talent might derive from the catastrophe of Jack's resentment, Wendy's weakness. Bettelheim's theory of autism has since been entirely discredited, and his take on the fairy tale has also been contested. In 1979, Angela Carter published *The Bloody Chamber*, a revision of classic fairy tales, unlocking the sexual energies of the original folk tales that had been suppressed by Victorian rewritings, and which implicitly challenged the idea that the tales were exercises in creating 'normal' children, conforming to conventional social mores. Her Red Riding Hood jumps into bed with the wolf (the book was filmed in 1984 by Neil Jordan as *The Company of Wolves*). The point of these primal tales is that by the late twentieth century they have become open grids of possibility, multiple chances for story, not merely moral homilies that can be reduced to singular interpretations.

Warner Bros.' maddening Bugs Bunny and the Road Runner lead from one kind of cartoon 'Looney Tune' in the classic 1940s era of Hollywood animation to another in *The Shining*. Perhaps those swoops across the mountain are not vengeful gods after all, but Wile E. Coyote running out past the edge of the cliff, keeping going until he realises that there is no ground beneath his feet.

Mirrored minds, mirrored hands

The conversation between the actors Scatman Crothers and Danny Lloyd in the kitchen took a legendary number of takes before Kubrick was satisfied. The discrimination of looks and pauses, the matching folded hands of man and boy, the lovely slip of Danny's reluctance to speak about the shining ('I'm not asposed to') are all worth waiting for. But perhaps we hang on to this scene because it is the last in the first movement of the film, the abrupt end of a social world, a place populated by others. From here on in, the Torrances have nothing but themselves to rely on in the vast catacomb of the Overlook.

## Daddy's in the doldrums

'A Month Later', 'Tuesday', 'Saturday', 'Wednesday', 'Monday, '4pm': Jack's descent into madness is managed rapidly, in a series of intertitles that telescope time and tighten the screw. In the first of these sequences, which are very similarly structured, Danny explores the Overlook in constant motion, gliding through hostile territory on his tricycle in slow loops. In contrast, Jack is rendered progressively immobile. First, he is still asleep at 11.30 in the morning and already on the other side of the looking glass. Kubrick films him in reverse within the constricting frame of the mirror (entirely so in the more rigorous UK cut of the scene), fending off Wendy's grating jollity about his writer's block with a set of sarcastic gestures and responses that barely maintain their civility. As Wendy and Danny set off at a run through the maze, Jack's typewriter is abandoned on a blank page and he furiously hurls a ball at the Diné mural above the fireplace. Bored, he looms over the model of the maze, conjuring a tiny wife and child at its heart, a startling trick shot created by shooting the centre of the maze from a high overhead rostrum camera and then matting the shot into the maze model. He is already tempted to regard himself as the master of his domain, his overlook the apparent perspective of power, an early identification with the forces of the hotel.

In 'Tuesday', the second sequence, Danny glides through the mazy patterns of the second floor, stops by Room 237, tries the

Danny's three loops

locked door, gets a single flash of the Grady girls and moves
concertedly away. Jack is seated at his desk, motionless but
hyperactive at the typewriter, his inspiration the cuttings book open
at his right hand. He is stricken at Wendy's gauche interruption.
The rage that has been suppressed from the beginning starts to show
itself, to Wendy's stilled dismay at his command: 'Why don't you
start right now and get the fuck out of here.' In the following scene,
as Wendy and Danny frolic through the heavy snow, Jack stands
immobile as a black monolith, his features utterly frozen, a man
entirely hollowed out, catatonic. That high-pitched sound associated
with the shining creeps into the soundtrack, and although we see
nothing supernatural, I wonder if it isn't the sound of Jack's empty
vessel being filled with the venom of the Overlook's history.

  In Danny's third, broken loop on his pedal car, the Grady sisters
stop him in his tracks and begin to whisper their promises to play for
ever and ever. Now the sisters are intercut with their slaughtered
bodies, axed down in the corridor but not yet neatly stacked in one
of the rooms. They have played their hand, though, those twins.
They are like the welcoming party. We never see them again. We see
nothing of Jack, because by the next sequence, 'Monday', he is

Jack as black monolith

caught in the classic signs of a debilitating depressive state. From oversleeping, he has become insomniac, trapped in a half-life between sleeping and waking, perched on the edge of the bed, stuck between resting or rising. As Danny enters the family quarters, he is caught between two Jacks, his father splintered between bed and mirror. The tender scene of father and son captures this doubleness: Jack's expression of love for Danny is undergirded with violent menace. The emptied Jack echoes the Grady girls – 'I wish we could stay here for ever and ever and ever' – clear evidence that he is fatally caught up in the matrix of the shining that stirs through the hotel.

In this middle portion of *The Shining*, the film empties Jack out; we have no access to his interior state. It is the opposite of the novel, which works to fill in his back-story, his childhood memories of his father's violent abuse, his brother's death in Vietnam, the oblivion of alcohol of the last few years, the pangs of his addiction. He works on the building; the organising metaphor of the novel is not the maze, but the wasps' nest, found in the roof, neutralised, but which comes to life again, and which figures the labyrinthine malignity of the hotel itself. King's Jack Torrance is a published writer of a dozen or so stories, seeking to finish a play. We have no evidence that Kubrick's

Jack Torrance has ever written anything. He is only waiting for something to occupy him, a blank slate on which the hotel can begin to write its own script.

This section of *The Shining* is a remarkable portrait of the depressive state: excessive sleep, turning into tormenting insomnia, withdrawal, blockage, devitalisation and eventually near catatonia – a becoming of what Christine Ross calls the depressed 'subject without others'. Another writer on depression has talked about the depressive state in art depicted as a cold world, 'the world in abeyance, in withdrawal', 'the vitalist world fallen into inert matter, the animist world deserted by its presiding spirits'.[23] The snowstorm, cutting the hotel off from all external communication, is the objective correlative of Jack's post-apocalyptic depressive world.

In passing, we should note the slightly alarming self-portrait of Kubrick that is suggested in this sequence. The typewriter on the desk is Kubrick's own, and we can see the director furiously typing away on a smaller portable, incorporating the last changes to the daily script, in the documentary on the making of *The Shining* that his daughter Vivian directed in 1980. Kubrick had a habit of throwing baseballs hard at the wall in the early days of scriptwriting, Vincent LoBrutto reports, frustrations that Jack Nicholson could also channel from his scripting years in the 1960s. Of course, the temptation is to read the retreat to the Overlook as a repetition of Kubrick's own progressive withdrawal into creative seclusion in the backwoods. And doesn't the endless repetition (with modulation) of the same line in Jack's writing recall the exasperation many felt with Kubrick's insistence on multiple, virtually identical takes?

But if this section of *The Shining* is about disconnection and withdrawal, it is only a passage in a film that formally and thematically is about occult communication and the weird connectedness that comes with telepathic transmission. When Jack gazes down on the model of the maze, magically fusing it with the original outside, we have an inkling of how Kubrick will link form and content to construct what could be called *telepathic cinema*.

By this, I mean the radical sense in which fluid transpositions actually dissolve the singular point of view for a sense of mobile and shared subjectivity. This ambition reaches its fruition in the scenes around the events inside Room 237, the enigmatic core of the whole film.

## Room 237

The scenes that lead up to and away from Room 237 are complexly choreographed. We encounter Lloyd the barman on either side of it, standing like a sentinel at the gates. The room is approached obliquely through Danny's shocked dissociative state, Dick Hallorann's trance vision and Jack's dream, the 'most terrible nightmare I ever had'. Room 237 is a rebus, operating through the condensations and displacements of dream-logic.

We could call Room 237 the navel of *The Shining*. In Freud's *The Interpretation of Dreams*, there is a particular dream to which he keeps returning because it stands as a challenge to his theory. A father in mourning for his son leaves the night watch over the corpse to snatch some sleep: he is awoken by a dream in which his son cries, 'Father, can't you see I'm burning?' The father awakes and rushes into the next room, to find that a candle has fallen over and set fire to

Jack's overlook

the corpse. Freud returns again and again to a dream that is at once too easy and too difficult to read. Whatever wish-fulfilment it reveals, it is also, symptomatically, a dream about a telepathic message from a dead child to his father. Is this where the metaphorical ghosts that float through dreams so absurdly, so nonchalantly, start to become literal? 'There is often a passage in even the most thoroughly interpreted dream which has to be left obscure,' Freud says. 'This is the dream's navel, the spot where it reaches down into the unknown.' Given Freud's obsession with dreams of the dead, with his constant references to the ghosts from *The Odyssey* 'which awoke to new life as soon as they tasted blood', it is not surprising that *The Interpretation of Dreams* has been called Freud's Gothic novel.[24]

The scene in Room 237 acts similarly as the navel of *The Shining*, at once easy to read and utterly obscure. The sequence impossibly intertwines the psychic lives of Wendy, Danny, Hallorann, Jack and the hotel. In this oneiric state, we enter a wholly new way of navigating cinematic intersubjectivity.

The sequence begins with what might be the ball that Jack threw down the corridor in the Colorado Lounge rolling to a stop in front of Danny on the floor above. He looks up at an empty corridor and vertiginously, in a single cut, the whole pattern of the carpet is turned 180 degrees, trapping Danny in its vicious pattern. His first response is to assume that the ball has been thrown by his mother, to whom he repeatedly calls out. The substitute for the mother is the open door of Room 237. Well, isn't the navel also the mark of your attachment to and detachment from the mother in the womb? From Danny's subjective point of view, we approach the open double door, the number 237 marked on the blood-red key fob, a last warning echo from the 'Bluebeard' story. We hear him ask, 'Mom, are you in there?' – and this is the moment when Danny winks out of existence, appearing for much of the rest of the film in a traumatised state as his dissociated alter ego Tony ('Danny's gone away, Mrs Torrance'). Whatever happens in there shocks him out of his being.

We cut to Wendy in the basement by the twin boilers, the only act of caretaking in the Overlook we ever see. She runs to Jack, hollering in his chair from the depths of his murderous nightmare. Her concern for Jack is interrupted by the arrival of Danny, seen across a huge depth of field, the whole length of the void of the Colorado Lounge. The bruises on Danny's neck and his wounded state finally tears asunder the fragile truce in the marriage. 'You did this to him, didn't you?' she accuses, barely able to carry the boy away to safety. Jack's own stricken state leaves him unable to respond to his wife, a denial whispered only after she has left. He leaves his self-defence to Lloyd at the bar of the Gold Room. He walks there, ranting and raving down the corridor like a far-gone street drinker with the DTs. The lights blink on in that impossible space, the bar swept clean. Jack is briefly doubled in the mirror behind the bar, from the place where Lloyd will appear. 'I'd give my goddamn soul for just a glass of beer', Jack mutters to the empty counters and shelves, and with this explicit Faustian pact, his fate is sealed. Lloyd is conjured into existence, hollowed eye sockets lit from below and with a glittering array of booze. Jack's confession, a scene that took over eighty takes before Kubrick was satisfied, is Nicholson at his mercurial best, emotions rushing across his face like the unstable weather system that circles so ominously outside. The gesture that recalls how he snaps the bone of his son is brilliant: at once a confession but a weasily refusal to speak it, a snap that turns into a contemptuous flinging away of any responsibility. He is damned by his delusion.

Is he merely dreaming? Wendy appears to nudge him awake as she enters an empty Gold Room to tell him that they are not alone: there's a crazy woman in one of the rooms that tried to strangle Danny. 'Are you out of your fucking mind?' he barks. If this is an alliance temporarily renewed, note that the wife is already carrying that baseball bat. 'Which room?' he asks with bullish confidence. And so we circle back to Room 237.

From whose perspective do we see the following sequence? This is impossible to answer. It starts, in a disorienting way, with a

jump-cut to a close-up of a Miami TV report, the camera pulling
out to reveal the perfect symmetry of the TV framed by two lamps,
two piles of records and two black feet. Hallorann lies on the bed
(two tutelary black nudes towering above him), watching reports of
the Colorado snow. In reverse, the camera pans in tightly on
Hallorann's face, his bottomless pupils, as a soundtrack heartbeat
and that high-pitched noise tell us we are entering a state of
telepathic vision.

Mercurial Jack, stormy weather at the Gold Room Bar

The confounding Room 237 sequence

A subjective shot lets us enter Room 237, woozily assess the horrific décor and push through the double bedroom door. Ahead, in an exact match of the layout of the family quarters, the bathroom door stands ajar. We assume at first that this is Danny's experience, time-slipped, conveyed to the cook through their shared ability to shine. In the novel, Dick tells the boy to send out a mental distress signal – a telepathic phantasm – if he ever gets into serious trouble, a scene that was actually filmed by a second unit and taken directly from the book, but which Kubrick did not use. Intercut are disturbing shots of Danny, seemingly in visionary, epileptic seizure, drooling at the mouth: but is this what he experienced (is he being strangled by a phantom?), is remembering or is projecting now at great psychic cost across the continent? But there is a jolting shift: the hand that pushes the door is not Danny's but his father's, repeating his son's investigation of the room. Is Danny then re-experiencing the scene through his father? The time sequence and point of view slips again. Jack's presence is only established once the woman behind the shower curtain has shifted, pulled the curtain back and revealed herself as a seductive nude. The reverse shot, sharing the viewpoint of the ghost, shows Jack's face turn from terror to slack-jawed desire. The young woman advances into a passionate embrace with Jack (the model, Lia Beldam, was plucked from screen tests for the Gold Room crowd scenes: she was on set for a week and didn't read the novel until later, not knowing quite what she was filming between her usual fashion shoots). The rotting corpse of a now much older woman that Jack embraces is only revealed – as ever – in the doubling mirror, the logic of dreams making desire turn to revulsion. The scene ends in disordered jump-cuts around this abject vision: she advances on an appalled Jack, but the film also cuts back to her rising from the bath (Danny's experience?), all under the crescendo of her mocking laughter. The heartbeat fades away: the circuit is closed by returning to Hallorann using the phone to begin his journey back to the Overlook through the storm.

This knot or navel of a scene ties together many viewpoints – it is the message received by Hallorann, Danny's traumatic experience or memory, Tony's preternatural vision, Jack's hallucination or the curdling into physical haunting of the hotel's malignant phantoms. Has this whole scene been impelled from some impossible 'objective' place by the 'orders of the house'? There is a kind of rapport, typical of hypnosis or trance states or experiences of traumatic extremity, that utterly dissolves the boundary between self and other, creating weird intersubjective states where point of view becomes confusingly unhooked from the self. This confusion of selves, of multiplication, uncanny repetition and the dissolution of boundaries, has always been what the Gothic has sought to achieve in its most delirious narratives. This is telepathy, too: the other in me, me in the other. And it is also Kubrick's uncanny cinema in *The Shining*, detaching point of view from any secure ground of identity.

As we have come to expect, this episode is also haunted by the history of horror, further complicating the sequence with other echoes and resonances. The whole delirious, dreamy feel of Room 237, horror set amidst the bold, clashing greens and purples of the set design, feels like a 1970s Dario Argento film, something like the heavily stylised *Suspiria* (1977), whose slashes of colour hide the cackling witch Madame Blanc at its secret heart. The shock of a female corpse rising from the bath evokes the sublime moment of terror in Henri-Georges Clouzot's *Les Diaboliques* (1955): a nasty trick designed to kill off the weak-hearted witness. Clouzot's misanthropy is shared in King's novel, where the woman in Room 217 (as it is in the book) is a self-piteous ageing vamp who commits suicide because her toy boy abandons her. Terror comes from inappropriate female desire, a perversion of the maternal figure that Danny calls out to at the very beginning of the sequence. Is the womb, the lost home, the unhomely site of horror? Is that the mother's heartbeat? Most obviously, though, this whole encounter is a kind of reverse of the foundational moment of modern horror: Marion's murder by Norman Bates in the

shower in *Psycho*. The perspective and power dynamic is inverted: *she* pulls the shower curtain back and advances on him, not vice versa; *she* is the one who is split between two different selves, not him. What Jack shares with Norman Bates is that both of them end up utterly unmanned.

To all this, we might observe that this scene also reverses the dynamic of Kubrick's other bathroom scene in *Lolita* (1962), where it is Shelley Winters who is the passive object of murderous thoughts.

Jack returns to the family quarters, issuing four denials: 'No. Nothing at all. I didn't see a goddamn thing. Absolutely nothing.' He seems too self-possessed to be lying: has he actually experienced nothing, then – this has been someone else's vision? Or has he, like his son, forgotten the moments of shining as soon as they are over? Jack works hard to transpose any blame. The truce ends abruptly when Wendy insists that they leave the hotel to take Danny to a doctor. As the emotional temperature ramps up between his

*Psycho* reversed

parents, Danny next door sees his first flash of REDRUM, the
psychic image that now replaces the Grady sisters, and the river of
blood from the lift. Jack storms back to the Gold Room, the hotel
coming alive around him, echoing to the sound of the 1920s band,
the corridor festooned with balloons. Danny's terror has boosted the
Overlook's psychic battery to a tipping point. The hotel's
insubstantial and timeless world, in which there is no difference
between life and death, or between present, past or future, takes on
physical presence.

A perfect symmetry is preserved. The same tracking shot used
twice before from the entrance moves along the edge of the Gold
Room to the bar, but this time it reveals a vast party of flappers and
dapper gents in full swing. This time, Lloyd the barman is there
waiting for Jack, serving up drinks for free. 'Orders from the house'
never had such an ominous ring.

## Mr Grady

Lloyd, we sense, is not a singular person: he is merely a conduit for
dark forces. And the waiter Delbert Grady is exactly the same.
The scene between Jack and Grady in the blood-red toilets (the
design inspired, it is said, by Frank Lloyd Wright's Biltmore Hotel)
continues the telepathic logic of merging and shifting identities.
The viewer is placed inside a rigorous logic of shot/reverse shot, used
to establish point of view in classical cinema, yet 'Mr Grady' is not a
person, but a panoply of ghosts. 'What do they call you round here,
Jeevesy?' Jack asks jocularly. To which the answer might come:
'My name is legion: for we are many.' This is uttered by a man,
the Gospel of Mark says, who arrives from the tombs 'with an
unclean spirit' occupied by many demons.[25]

Delbert Grady is the apologetic, deferential servant, dabbing at
Jack's ruined jacket. He has a wife and two daughters, he says, but
he is perhaps right to politely refuse being called the axe-murderer
who killed his family and then blew his own brains out.
Ullmann names *that* caretaker as Charles Grady in the opening

How many Gradys are there in this bathroom?

interview. The slip is surely deliberate, sowing confusion, slyly multiplying identities, giving a sense that in the timeless time of the hotel there is an endless chain of atrocity enacted over and over again. The camera remains entirely static during these exchanges, shifting from establishing shot to mid-shot to the shot/reverse shot of dialogue, but by the time Grady is given his close-up, he is no longer the servant but the iron-willed voice of paternal authority. His words, lifted virtually verbatim from King's novel, are chilling. He seeks Jack's complicity by using a racist slur, warning that a 'nigger cook' is being called on to interfere in the situation. Jack's hesitant repetition of the taboo word 'nigger' shows him already half-willing to appease. His eyes slide sideways, anxious yet childishly thrilled with a taboo transgressed. By now, Delbert Grady has certainly become Charles Grady, asserting that wilful children need 'a good talking to, if you don't mind my saying so. Perhaps a bit more.' He speaks of his daughters' resistance to the Overlook. 'I corrected them, sir,' Grady says of them. 'And when my wife tried to prevent me from doing my duty, I corrected her.' Philip Stone's crisp English accent, heavy on the hard 'c', gives Grady's euphemism a menacing twist, like a term Goebbels might have used to evade the realities of mass murder in the concentration camps. In the red room, identity slides vertiginously on Grady's side of the conversation. No wonder when his iron voice speaks unseen through the storeroom door, he says, 'I and others have come to believe that your heart is not in this.' 'I and others': he is legion; he is many.

It is often said that Kubrick veers between two extreme styles of acting: a kind of numbed, blank mode typical of the astronauts in *2001* or Ryan O'Neal in *Barry Lyndon*, and the exaggerated, expressionist style of Peter Sellers as Dr Strangelove or Patrick Magee in *A Clockwork Orange*. The face-off between Philip Stone and Jack Nicholson brings these two clashing styles together. It is the stillness of Stone's performance that amplifies the expressionist tones of Nicholson's portrayal; it is the launch pad for Nicholson to lose his restraint, and explode.

### 'How do you like it?': Jack goes ape

Wendy cradles the empty shell of her son, who is busy imbibing more
TV lessons from *Road Runner*. She ventures downstairs to talk to
Jack. The Colorado Lounge is empty; she walks the length of it,
cradling the baseball bat, and passes into the shadows beyond the
writing desk. The music of Penderecki swells on the soundtrack – it
will be an insistent presence for the remainder of the film.
Wendy returns to the desk, the cuttings book resting by the
typewriter. The shot from the point of view of the typewriter up to
her face allows an extraordinary reveal: her stricken reaction to what
appears to be the completed manuscript that Jack has been working
on. 'All work and no play makes Jack a dull boy.' (In the age of
micro-publishing, Jack's novel has now of course been published.
I often wonder idly that if Jack is locked in a cycle of eternal
repetition, did he also write this book in the hotel in 1921? If so, it
has clearly been inspired by a reading of Apollinaire's concrete poetry
in *Calligrammes*, which appeared in 1918. Jack's book resembles,
but precedes, the great works of modernism's miracle year, 1922.
*All Work and No Play* anticipates some of Gertrude Stein's most
extreme experiments: it is a lost modernist masterpiece.)

The screen goes briefly black, before the camera emerges from
that dark spot behind the desk, shifting right to left, watching Wendy
crouched over the desk from behind. Jack's silhouette emerges out of
this darkness and into frame – Wendy is shot from over his shoulder,
but once again with an ominous feeling that the point of view is no
longer simply Jack's but multiple and increasingly menacing.
'How do you like it?' he asks.

In this moment, we know there is no way back for their
marriage, and the story will only end badly. Jack moves aggressively
forward, pushing Wendy back towards the stairs, the space of a bat
swing between them. He is amped, jittery, his gestures exaggerated,
the mocking imitations of his wife grotesque. As she backs onto the
stairs, she starts swinging the bat in front of her. 'Light of my life!'
he says, echoing Humbert Humbert from *Lolita*, as he taunts

Wendy. 'I'm not going to hurt you – I'm just gonna bash your fucking brains out!'

From this point, Nicholson's performance leaps off the deep end for the rest of the film. It started with satanic eyebrow action – from here, it can only get louder and brasher. Kubrick encouraged improvisation, and it would produce Nicholson's most famous,

'How do you like it?'; irreconcilable differences

parodied line as he hacks the bathroom door down: 'Heeere's Johnny!' as if he were a demented talk-show host. These scenes took hours of exhausting retakes. The baseball-bat scene, it has been said, took 127 takes alone. What do you make of this performance? How do you like it?

There were rumours that Nicholson was worried through the year-long shoot that Kubrick was pushing for too broad and exaggerated a style, and that the ripest versions of his lines buried in the endless retakes were the ones Kubrick had chosen. It feeds the view, held by many of Kubrick's detractors, that the director cared little for actors, thinking only of abstract bodies distributed in space, captured to technical perfection. This was Pauline Kael's consistent humanist objection to his films, although one might argue that if Kubrick's theme is anti-human systems that have trapped man, then this approach to acting perfectly fits his theme. Allies of Kubrick, like the critic Michel Ciment, argue precisely the opposite: Kubrick rehearsed with his actors on film, in actual takes, working in unique collaboration with them to generate the most effective cinematic route through the script – he was devoted to acting. To Vivian Kubrick, Nicholson claimed that he longed to pass the reading of his performance over to a strong director like Kubrick: 'I want to be out of control.'

Nicholson's arch performance in *The Shining* descends from the exaggerated expressionism Kubrick used in many of his satires, most obviously *Dr Strangelove* and *A Clockwork Orange*. Nicholson is directed in exactly the same way as Patrick Magee in the later stages of *Orange* – indeed, it's almost as if Jack Torrance climbs out of the face of Mr Alexander. For those who read *The Shining* as less a horror film than a parody of horror, the performance is meant to be a subversion of the unstable shift between 'bloody terror and carnivalistic comedy' typical of the genre.[26] Nicholson had early training in horror ham from working as the straight man to no less a trio than Boris Karloff, Peter Lorre and Vincent Price in Roger Corman's *The Raven* (1963).

This is a weak defence, though, and I tend to think that there is a certain integrity to Nicholson's escalating hysteria in *The Shining*. Nicholson was clearly drawn to portraits of conflicted masculinity in the 1970s: in Bob Rafelson's *Five Easy Pieces* or Antonioni's *The Passenger* (1975), both men are anxious to escape constricting identities. Institutional systems bring down Jake Gittes in *Chinatown* (1974) and McMurphy in *One Flew over the Cuckoo's Nest* (1975). Of *The Shining*, Nicholson said: 'I play the character as a guy who's deeply pathological in the area of his marital relationships. The book had that intimation to begin with, and then I just blew it up.'[27] His favoured pattern has been narratives of constraint leading to explosion, up to and including *About Schmidt* (2002), where the audience is left comically aware that the inevitable explosion of rage will come, it's just a matter of when. By the time Jack picks up the axe in *The Shining*, constraint has played out, but it is significant that his performance from this point is almost exclusively citational, as if to demonstrate that the Overlook has finally hollowed him out and all he can do is quote. He steals a line from Humbert Humbert. He tickles the locked door of the storeroom with his fingers like Oliver Hardy. He limps like the hump-backed assistant Fritz in the original *Frankenstein* (1931), wonderfully parodied by Marty Feldman as Igor in *Young Frankenstein* (1974). He intones the bedtime story of the 'Three Little Pigs'. He is a demonic Johnny Carson. And 'Wendy, I'm home' is of course stolen from Ricky Ricardo's catchphrase in *I Love Lucy*, chosen to subvert that jolly 1950s family sitcom. It is a performance in keeping with the logic of Jack's dethronement. It is not simply a continuation of the gurning that marred his role in the self-directed *Goin' South* (1978), but carefully considered.

Of course, Nicholson's stardom spills over into the role of Jack Torrance and sets up all kinds of resonances within the scenario. What echoes here is not just his association with counter-cultural rebellion, but the immediate crisis that had engulfed his Hollywood circle. It was in Nicholson's house that Roman Polanski was arrested

Antic Jack

in 1977 for sex with a minor, before fleeing America in 1978; it was his then girlfriend, Angelica Huston, who was also briefly arrested for possession of drugs. Nicholson's own immediate family – both the identity of his mother and father – had been thrown into doubt with newspaper revelations in 1974. Nicholson spoke in these years of a conspiracy by the Family Values movement on the newly emergent Republican right against prominent counter-cultural libertarians like himself. A year in England shooting *The Shining* got him away from this paranoid and unhappy world, but it perhaps also spills into the performance too.

In retrospect, *The Shining* seems like a threshold in Nicholson's career, a role that for many trapped him in self-parody. We have to watch *The Shining* back through the performances in the 1980s that fixed this stereotype: Daryl Van Horne in *The Witches of Eastwick* (1987) or The Joker in Tim Burton's *Batman* (1989), in which he essentially plays the character 'Jack Nicholson from *The Shining*'. It is not really Nicholson's fault that *The Shining* is viewed through the lens of his subsequent performances, yet it is impossible not to watch the Kubrick film and see in the last act the form of a fixed persona taking shape.

### Polymorphia: the sound of *The Shining*
One of the greatest successes of *The Shining* is its extraordinary soundscape and score, which is a major contribution to the film's eerie and confounding tone. The film itself is structured like a piece of music, with large movements, recurring rhythms and melodic fragments that bind different scenes together in echo and repetition that reinforce the sense of the uncanny. It is most closely related to Kubrick's score for *2001*, which, as Alex Ross has observed, 'neatly brackets the entire arc of twentieth-century musical history' by beginning with Richard Strauss's *Thus Spake Zarathustra* and ending with György Ligeti's post-war experimentalism in the 'catastrophe style'.[28] *The Shining* also proceeds from the opening plangent chords of the *Dies Irae*, mockingly reworked by Hector Berlioz in 1830,

through the work of the Hungarian exile from Nazism Béla Bartók from the 1930s, Ligeti's experiments in 'texture music' in the 50s, and culminating in six pieces taken from the Polish composer Krzysztof Penderecki, mainly from the 60s, including the complete score of his notorious work, *Polymorphia*.

Against this relentless modernism, the distorted echoes of Ray Noble and His Orchestra playing 'Midnight, the Stars and You' bathes the Gold Room in woozy, soporific nostalgia. As Delbert Grady icily commands Jack in the blood-red men's room, the jazz band plays a song called 'Home', of dangerous allure to Jack's faltering ego.

Very early in the film's development, Kubrick asked the composer Wendy Carlos to read Stephen King's book and produce some sample electronic scoring (as she had done for *A Clockwork Orange*). The result was a double album of material, created long before she had seen any images, most of which was never used in the final film except for the title sequence *Dies Irae*. Her sound composition 'Shining/Heartbeat' recurs throughout the film as one of the signature noises of telepathic communion, a high-pitched buzzing with heartbeat pulse combined with Rachel Elkind's vocal embellishments.

In the opening movement of the film, Ligeti's *Lontano* recurs three times, the first accompanying Danny's vision of the twins in the Games Room. This short orchestral piece was an experiment in what became known as 'micropolyphony', a dense clustering and overlay of tones from all the instruments at once that produces a sort of persistent buzzing effect, deliberately setting the nerves on edge in the higher registers. One liner note memorably describes Ligeti as using the timbres of air-raid sirens. For another critic, the hovering of these sounds is 'vast and ominous', the noise of the 'hopelessness of elapsing time'.[29] I sometimes wonder if this buzzing is the sound of the wasps' nest, so central to the novel but missing from the film. It is as if the insect music was meant to evoke the hive mind of the Overlook Hotel, agitated with inhuman intelligence.

It is risky but tempting to read Ligeti's biography into this catastrophe music: a Transylvanian Jew whose father and brother were killed in concentration camps, and who also suffered persecution under the Stalinist regime in Hungary until he fled to Austria in 1956. He once described his piercing tones as repeated stabs in Stalin's heart. Without doubt, this music is the sound of distress, a kind of strickenness that is the only soundtrack imaginable to accompany such disaster. It slides under the early scenes of *The Shining* with a sense of dread, dragging the atrocities of the twentieth century with it.

Bartók's *Music for Strings, Percussion and Celesta* (composed in 1936) also recurs several times in the first forty minutes (for instance, as Danny and Wendy enter the hedge maze), a piece recognisable by its persistent, tapping percussion and distorted, nauseous rolls on the tympanum. Bartók was in the early years of his exile from Hungary, a political opponent of fascism who saw the writing on the wall. Disaster also lurks in this music. Unlike the dense clustering of Ligeti, this is a piece full of menace in its lugubrious movement, long pauses and wide spaces.

In an important way, the film moves from intermittent musical elements to a frenetic final movement in which every action is orchestrated to a thunderous, emphatic, crashing score (sometimes too emphatic for my taste). The last forty minutes of the film are dominated by the music of Penderecki, the Polish experimentalist who further developed Ligeti's adventures in micropolyphony. Throughout the film, Kubrick's music editor, Gordon Stainforth, extensively manipulated elements of Penderecki's music, layering and cutting between *De Natura Sonoris*, *Kanon for Orchestra and Tape* and other pieces. In an ingenious way, which only adds to the enigma of the Room 237 sequence, the Wendy Carlos signature 'Heartbeat/ Shining' is also layered with Penderecki's 1974 piece *The Awakening of Jacob*, a densely polychromatic work inspired by the line in the book of Genesis, 'Jacob awoke from his sleep and said: Truly the Lord is in this place, and I did not know it.' The telepathic binding

Penderecki's score for *Polymorphia*

around the 237 sequence is extended by the resonances set up by the music of Penderecki, a composer who first came to notice for the catastrophe music of *Threnody to the Victims of Hiroshima*. Typically, Kubrick was happy to heavily manipulate and snip the music, editing it to the rhythm of the visual cut (Ligeti sued Kubrick for lack of permission and distortion of his music in *2001*, a mistake the director rectified by giving full credit in *The Shining*).

However, unlike the extensive use of sampling in most scenes, Penderecki's 1961 piece *Polymorphia* is played in full. It is the culminating piece of music in *The Shining*, and if it sounds like the soundtrack of the modern horror film, perhaps that is because it was first used in *The Exorcist* and has subsequently been heard in David

Lynch's *Inland Empire* (2006). It is now encoded in the culture as the music of existential dread. It sounds like nothing else: tonal clusters of notes urged along, sliding through weird glissandi, until it reaches a clatter of percussive tappings and thuds. The instruction to the strings is to play *legno battuto*, that is to strike the strings with the wooden back of the bow. In this piece, the instruments are not so much played as attacked. It sounds like a horde of insects eating their way out of the string section.

*Polymorphia* initially bubbles up under the first open argument between Jack and Wendy, playing all the way through the staircase scene and beyond into the sequence where Wendy drags Jack's body to the storeroom. Christine Lee Gengaro's invaluable study of the music in *The Shining* traces just how the complex overlays of different pieces are built up in the film in a kind of meta-micropolyphony, but *Polymorphia* alone dominates this sequence. In the last scenes, when the psychic hotel has become so amplified that even Wendy begins to see the ghosts, Kubrick emphasises each shock with a loud percussive burst, symbol crashes matching crash zooms, borrowed from Penderecki's religious choral piece, *Utrenja*. It is significant that Gengaro calls these moments 'stings' – precisely as if it is insect bites that punctuate these shock moments: the body of Hallorann, the skeletons in the lobby, the blood from the lift. It completes the musical trajectory of the film towards ever more declarative, emphatic sounds; the return of 'Midnight, the Stars and You' over the last shot and the closing credits is the bitterly ironic calm after the storm.

In a perceptive early response to the film, Paul Mayersberg commented that *The Shining* was essentially like post-war avant-garde music: 'technically brilliant and yet fundamentally heartless'. Melody and tonality had been under attack since Schoenberg's acts of war against harmony in the 1910s. Mayersberg suggests that Ligeti's music 'has a mocking tone as if laughing at all past music and at people with notions of fixed values'.[30] Yet avant-garde music was also changing in the 1970s, stepping back from the most radically atonal work to find new associations with forbidden melody. Once again, the soundtrack reinforces the sense of *The Shining* as the film of a transitional time. Its mixed musical range accorded with Kubrick's wish to remain within the Hollywood machinery whilst pushing its technical and narrative conventions to the very limit.

## The 'Magical Negro': Hallorann

Jack has gone ape, smashing at the bathroom door with his trusty axe. But his ranting, Wendy's screaming and the screeching score drop away at a far-off alien noise: the sound of Hallorann arriving in the Sno-Cat. The family romance will have to be put on hold.

Poor Scatman Crothers. The sixty-nine-year-old veteran actor, who had already appeared in three films with Nicholson in the 1970s (when I spent most of my time listening to him as the voice of the cartoon character Hong Kong Phooey), was killed forty times with that axe. Nicholson pleaded with Kubrick to wrap up the takes, to save his old friend more draining physical effort.

Poor Hallorann. He travels selflessly across a continent, journeys through the storm and up the mountain to the Overlook Hotel, only to take one in the chest within minutes of arriving. This is not how it ends in the novel. As so often in King stories, the benign black man survives and becomes the substitute father. Hallorann is badly injured by Jack (as is Wendy), but he gets Wendy and Danny down the mountain, and the epilogue is set in the western Maine mountains, where the survivors form a post-traumatic sort-of family unit.

In the film, Hallorann is reduced to a valet service, providing only the means of escape. Even worse, he conforms to a stereotypical Hollywood role that has become known as the 'Magical Negro'. This explosive phrase was introduced into discussion of Hollywood cinema at around the time of the success of another Stephen King adaptation, *The Green Mile* (1999). The Magical Negro is the decidedly minor black character, surrounded by an aura of spirituality or actual supernatural power, who serves as a sacrificial helper to the white hero, providing the means for white advance often through their own death. Classical Hollywood consolidated this figure in *The Defiant Ones* (1958), where Sidney Poitier sacrifices himself to let Tony Curtis escape. But some commentators were particularly incensed by a cluster of films that renewed this figure, including *The Green Mile*, *The Legend of Bagger Vance* (2000) and *Family Man* (2000). Spike Lee was contemptuous of what he saw as a recycling of the noble savage stereotype.

The writer Nnedi Okorafor-Mbachu also observed that the Magical Negro was a recurring figure in several Stephen King novels, whether it was Mother Abigail in *The Stand* (1978) and Speedy Parker in *The Talisman* (1984), or the telepathic Dick Hallorann, whose homespun term 'the shining' was learned from his silent communions with his grandmother. It has become such a cliché that in the fourth season of the *Venture Brothers* cartoon (2009), the father explains wearily to his son: 'Not all black men have the shining'.[31]

The Magical Negro is intended as a gesture of benign liberal inclusion, but it tends only to reinforce racial imbalance. There is an implicit equation between the telepathic young child and the black man in *The Shining* (in their mirrored postures at the kitchen table), which equates their 'primitive' state and suggests that telepathy is a power associated with subordinated people. Indeed, Victorian psychical researchers often firmly believed that primitive races were more able to use telepathy, a force repressed by civilisation. In the film, what the black figure does is define the shining as a tactic of the oppressed against the lethal force of the 'white manhood' of American authority: the counter-force will come from an alliance of the marginal and overlooked – the black man, the child and the mother. Yet even Kubrick's most sympathetic critics tend to be a little embarrassed by the dismissive treatment of the figure of Hallorann, whom he patronisingly calls 'a simple, rustic type' in his conversation with Michel Ciment.[32]

## Wendy shines

And poor Shelley Duvall. In the novel, Wendy Torrance finds inner resources to protect her son and even re-establishes a family unit divested of patriarchal violence. She knows there is something uncanny about her son; she can be fiercely protective; she can express desire. Diane Johnson wrote a substantial role for Wendy in the film (Johnson's complex portrayal of a paranoid, persecuted mother in her novel *The Shadow Knows* gives a clue to how this might have been). But Kubrick persistently cut Wendy's role back in the screenwriting process and even further on set. She becomes a weak, reactive wife, whose masochism only incites Jack's sadism to ever greater heights, a toxic symbiosis.

Duvall's gangly frame and extraordinary face – pale skin framed by jet black hair, protruding eyes emphasised by make-up and lighting – are the prime locus where horror is registered in the film. Although the parodists focus on Nicholson's antics on the other side of the bathroom door, it is actually Duvall's intense performance, trapped in the corner, aghast, her body echoed by the shape of the knife she holds, which always impresses me. David Thomson said that Duvall 'resembles a hapless amateur dumped down in a star part': he's wrong.[33] Her awkwardness with the doctor, during the hotel tour or as a wife chivvying a fragile husband along is superb acting. Even the forest ranger at the other end of the CB radio sounds exasperated with the banality of her stumbling conversation: he looks down as if he's restraining himself from lashing out.

In Vivian Kubrick's documentary footage of her father at work, it is clear that he treated Duvall much as Jack treats Wendy in the narrative: with an insidious, undercutting bullying. 'It looks false, Shelley, I'm telling you.' 'Don't sympathise with her,' he says menacingly to the assistants around her, 'it doesn't help.' He loses his temper when she misses a cue; she looks like a chastened schoolgirl. Nicholson also ostentatiously ignores her in this footage, as if he has caught the same vibe. Yet it was Duvall who had just won joint Best

Actress at Cannes in 1977 for Robert Altman's *Three Women*. It's as if Kubrick wants to knock her stuffing out. In her early review, Pauline Kael acutely observed: 'We can feel that she's held down; she usually brings a more radiant eccentricity to her parts.'[34]

Yet Duvall understood that this was a game to enhance her performance, a 'butting of heads', she said, 'that was a necessary turmoil'. She understood the dynamic. To keep that hysteria going for so many takes, resentment and anger was necessary fuel.

Duvall shines; Wendy shines

Kubrick did not write films for women: perhaps Nicole Kidman alone had something approaching a complex part from the director, but even *Eyes Wide Shut* (1999) decides not to follow her story in the end. Duvall's acting is one of the best female performances in the Kubrick canon, a brilliantly skittish wife seeking approval from exasperated men. All the same, Duvall retreated to some extent from acting and into producing in the 1980s and 90s, as if the trauma of working with Kubrick had powerful lasting effects.

Wendy is the last to catch the shine of the hotel. When she leaves the bathroom, hunting for Danny in the maze of the Overlook, even her dulled capacities begin to sense things, to hear the chanting voices, and to see the memory traces of events from the hotel's past. She has a tacky imagination, perhaps, but then, as her husband says, she is a 'confirmed ghost story and horror film addict'. At the top of the stairs, she sees a 'bestial' act of fellatio performed on a man by another dressed in a pig mask. Below, she turns to see a man with a skull cracked just where she had hit Jack with the baseball bat: 'Great party, isn't it?' he asks politely. These are traces left over from the culminating masque conjured up in King's novel. However, it is Kubrick's idea alone (only in the US version) that Wendy runs into the foyer which is full of cobwebby skeletons. There is even a butler

'Great party, isn't it?'

there, serving drinks, perhaps a hint that this is meant to be Delbert Grady. For me, this is a bum note, a cheap-jack Gothic that even Corman would avoid – and it was a good decision to cut it from the shorter version. Most significantly, though, the wave of blood from the lift is finally attached to a person. The vision, the image Danny (and the audience of the teasing trailers, six months before the release) has seen from the very first, is witnessed by his mother, at the moment of her greatest extremity. It marks the sense that the power of the Overlook Hotel has reached its full force: that it can enfold anyone into its psychic world now.

## The maze and the minotaur

In the final chase, through the kitchen and out into the maze, Danny's roving explorations of the hotel allow him to best his father, to frustrate Jack's murderous Oedipal fantasy but fulfil his own. The Steadicam snaps at Danny's heels, making the hedges loom higher, the footsteps in the snow a fatal trace that will become his rescue, the Ariadne thread leading him not only out of the maze but out of his trance state too, and back into the arms of his mother, a full being again. Jack, hollowed out of any subjectivity now, howling at the moon, is the minotaur in the labyrinth. As Ovid's *Metamorphosis* records the myth:

Within this labyrinth Minos shut fast
The beast, half bull, half man, and fed him twice
On Attic blood, lot-chosen each nine years
Until the third choice mastered him. The door,
So difficult, which none of those before
Could find again, by Ariadne's aid
Was found, the thread that traced the way rewound.[35]

Danny, the 'third choice' after Grady's daughters, has the intelligence to escape Daedalus's labyrinth. But in cutting away the epilogue that focused on the survivors, Kubrick's interest is really

only in the grand metaphysical statement of Jack's entrapment
and death in the maze. 'The Minotaur, by his very being, opens a
second labyrinth', the French writer Michel Foucault once mused:
'the entrapment of man, beast, and the gods, a knot of appetites and
mute thoughts'.[36]

    The maze is the dominant symbol of *The Shining*, replacing
Stephen King's topiary creatures, which exploited more primal
animistic fears and come fully alive in the final sections of the book

Theseus and the Minotaur

(Kubrick's decision to abolish the topiary, even before CGI technology made this remotely possible, is fully vindicated in the risible green beasts of the TV mini-series in 1998). Instead, Kubrick multiplies the emblem of the maze in maps, models, broken pathways through the hotel, in the carpet patterns, in the twists and turns in the kitchen, and in the Navajo designs. There were two mazes built on set, one outdoors for the initial exploration by Wendy and Danny, one inside for the final chase sequences. The crew got repeatedly lost, to Kubrick's immense frustration: challenged by his small team, Kubrick promptly got lost as well.

As his wife and child lumber away in the Sno-Cat to safety, Wendy tossing away the phallic knife, Jack's turns in the maze get smaller and smaller until he stalls. The last musical 'sting' comes with the jump-cut to Jack's frozen body, stiff and dead in the snow the next morning, his eyes upturned to the mocking gods who overlook his fate. It is perhaps an echo of the last shots of Altman's *McCabe and Mrs Miller* (1971), in which large corporate forces eventually circle and snuff out McCabe in the snowy wastes on the outskirts of town.

But it is a fate that perfectly exemplifies Kubrick's own philosophical stance. It is a pessimistic account of the human failure ever to escape the ineluctable forces that entrap men. Plans will always go awry (as the heist does in *The Killing*); technological systems will always dethrone the humans that design them (as in *Dr Strangelove* or *2001*); family is not a retreat but a sprung trap (*Barry Lyndon*, *Eyes Wide Shut*, *The Shining*). Kubrick's heroes, Robert Kolker argues, are always defeated 'by the rituals and structures they set up for themselves'.[37]

The Surrealist philosopher Georges Bataille uses the metaphor of the labyrinth to argue a similar idea, that 'a man is only a particle inserted in unstable and entangled wholes', where Being is distributed in a confounding way, and never sovereign.[38] Twentieth-century horror is secular in a way the Gothic is not, because the Gothic clings to a Christian metaphysic of good and evil, justice and punishment.

Kubrick inspects the set of the Colorado Lounge destroyed by fire

Secular horror instead offers a glimpse of the absolute black nothingness that lies beneath the maze of appearances, a revelation that there is no transcendent reality, only the final death of meaning. Weirdly enough, this European philosophy of negation, fuelled by the atrocities of that century of extremes, was once criticised by the Marxist critic Georg Lukács, who said intellectuals had seemingly taken up residence in the Grand Hotel Abyss, 'a beautiful hotel, equipped with every comfort, on the edge of the abyss, of nothingness, of absurdity'.[39] This is an exact description of Kubrick's Overlook Hotel, astride of the grave and awaiting the wrath of the mountain gods.

What Stephen King most seemed to dislike about the film was that the fire that destroyed the Overlook in the novel had been converted into an isolated death by ice. This was to King a precise figuration of Kubrick's cold indifference in the end to human suffering. But did King know that sound-stage 3 had been destroyed overnight by fire six months before the end of shooting, eating up the Colorado Lounge and causing delays that cost the production $2.5 million?

In a film of doubles, mirrors and splittings, it seems only appropriate that the Overlook Hotel is defeated by both fire and ice.

## The photograph

The final shot is the slow dolly towards the photograph that contains Jack Torrance at a party on 4 July 1921 (a parricidal date, a date that shakes off the old colonial father). It is centred in an array of twenty-one images, just beyond the foyer on the way to the Gold Room, a distracting red sofa that has been sitting there the entire film now removed to make you focus on the image. Typically, Kubrick took a week to film this shot, as he obsessively ironed out imperceptible bumps on the dolly. Two dissolves bring us into tight close-up on the fresh-faced, Gatsby-like figure of Jack Torrance. What is the piece of paper that Jack holds in his hand? Why is the man behind him trying to pull it away, out of sight of the camera? 'Midnight, the Stars and You' plays again, a nostalgic afterglow. Once the epilogue was snipped out, this became the final image of the film.

It is an enigmatic way to end. What are we meant to think? Is it a final triumph of the occult power of the hotel, finally absorbing another victim into its history? If so, it would be an echo of the array of photographs seen at the end of *Burnt Offerings*, images of the successive families that have hired and become victims of the mansion. Or is it less a debt to horror film than another cheap joke ending, borrowed from a *Twilight Zone* episode, a last contemptuous mockery of the horror genre?

Perhaps it is more metaphysical than that, making us wonder if Jack Torrance had been there all along. Jack tells Wendy he experienced overwhelming déjà vu when he first arrived at the Overlook. It makes sense of Delbert Grady's insistence that 'You've *always* been the caretaker. I should know, I've *always* been here.' Each time you watch the film after this, you will pause the DVD and peer to see if you can catch this photograph from the corner of your eye (you never can).

Perhaps it is meant to come with the force of Nietzsche's idea of eternal recurrence. 'What if', Nietzsche asked in *The Gay Science*, 'a demon crept after you one day or night in your loneliest solitude and said to you: "This life, as you live it now and have lived it, you

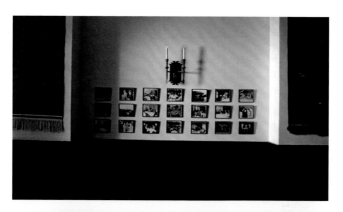

The final enigma

will have to live again and again, times without number"?'[40] But in Nietzsche's writing, this is not meant to be the prologue to damnation, quite the opposite: it is Nietzsche's affirmation of *amor fati*, the embrace of one's fate, that one would choose to live one's life just as it is, with all its highs and lows, over and over. Kubrick would have to be mocking such a welcoming of eternal return.

Then again, this can't be a direct repetition, can it? This is not the photograph of a janitor but one of those jet-set-before-the-jet-set playboys. This is Jack the celebrity, an F. Scott Fitzgerald in his pomp, not the later Fitzgerald, a struggling alcoholic. Fredric Jameson suggested in an early interpretation that we read this as the return to the last confident moment of class and race hierarchy in America in the 1920s, a response to the economic and social instabilities of the 70s that arguably helped foster the horror boom in the first place. The Overlook is America's past glory, frontier-triumphant, however bathed in blood. It is Rob Ager's theory that the people immediately surrounding Jack Torrance in the photograph are Woodrow Wilson, his wife and daughter – a proposal that might underpin such a reading, if only the likenesses were more persuasive!

I actually think Stephen King's plot trajectory holds more ethical force than Kubrick's insistence on circularity: King's novel shows an early awareness of what would become understood as cycles of physical and mental abuse, passed down from father to son in the American family. This is a rhythm that is decisively broken by the death of Jack Torrance (however sentimentally handled). But Kubrick is rigorous enough to resist being discursive at this point, and his philosophy would never have gelled with King's fragile optimism for cautious rebirth. Circularity, by definition, refuses to force an ending. Instead, the last shot is a recursive revelation that demands an instant reviewing of the film to hunt for clues. And so we watch it again. And again. We have been stuck in the loop of Kubrick's mesmerising maze of a movie ever since.

# Notes

**1** Pauline Kael, 'Devolution', in *Taking It All In* (London: Marion Boyars, 1986), pp. 6, 2 and 1; P. L. Titterington, 'Kubrick and *The Shining*', *Sight & Sound* (February 1981), p. 117.

**2** De Palma, quoted in Dennis Bingham, 'The Displaced Auteur: A Reception History of *The Shining*', in Mario Falsetto (ed.), *Perspectives on Stanley Kubrick* (New York: G. K. Hall, 1996), p. 285.

**3** Stephen King, quoted in Vincent LoBrutto, *Stanley Kubrick* (London: Faber, 1997), p. 409; King, *Danse Macabre* (London: Hodder, 1981), p. 245.

**4** Vincent Canby, quoted in Bingham, 'Displaced Auteur', p. 304.

**5** Paul Mayersberg, 'The Overlook Hotel', in Falsetto (ed.), *Perspectives on Stanley Kubrick*, pp. 256–7.

**6** H. P. Lovecraft, *Supernatural Horror in Literature* (New York: Dover, 1973), p. 60.

**7** Shirley Jackson, *Novels and Stories* (New York: Library of America, 2010), p. 417.

**8** King, cited by Kate Egan, *The Evil Dead* (London: Wallflower Press, 2011), p. 20.

**9** Robin Wood, *Hollywood from Vietnam to Reagan* (New York: Columbia University Press, 1986), pp. 50, 69, 75, 93.

**10** David Thomson, *Overexposures: The Crisis in American Filmmaking* (New York: Morrow, 1981), p. 333.

**11** William Paul, *Laughing, Screaming: Modern Hollywood Horror and Comedy* (New York: Columbia University Press, 1994), p. 307.

**12** Definition from glossary of terms at front of F. W. H. Myers, *Human Personality and Its Survival of Bodily Death*, two vols. (London: Longmans, 1903), p. xix.

**13** F. W. H. Myers, 'The Subliminal Consciousness', *Proceedings of the Society for Psychical Research*, vol. 11 (1895), chapter 8, p. 405.

**14** Michel Ciment, *Kubrick* (London: Collins, 1983), p. 181.

**15** V. I. Pudovkin, *Film Technique and Film Acting*, ed. Ivor Montague (London: Vision, 1968), pp. 24–5.

**16** David Cooper, *The Death of the Family* (Harmondsworth: Penguin, 1971), pp. 5, 6, 11.

**17** Sigmund Freud, 'Family Romances' (1909), in *Standard Edition of the Complete Psychological Works*, vol. IX (London: Hogarth Press, 1959), pp. 237, 239.

**18** Sigmund Freud, 'From the History of an Infantile Neurosis: The "Wolf Man"' (1918), in *Case Histories II*, *Penguin Freud Library*, vol. IX (Harmondsworth: Penguin, 1981), p. 273.

**19** Leslie Fiedler, *Love and Death in the American Novel* (Champaign, IL: Dalkey Archive, 1998), p. 135.

**20** Geoffrey Cocks, 'Stanley Kubrick, the Holocaust and *The Shining*', in Cocks et al. (eds), *Depth of Field: Stanley Kubrick, Film, and the Uses of History* (Madison: University of Wisconsin Press, 2006), p. 185.

**21** Thomas Allen Nelson, *Kubrick: Inside a Film Artist's Maze* (Bloomington: Indiana University Press, 1982), pp. 14–15.

**22** Bruno Bettelheim, *The Uses of Enchantment: The Meaning and Importance of Fairy Tales* (London: Penguin, 1991), pp. 7, 42, 302.

**23** Christine Ross, *The Aesthetics of Disengagement: Contemporary Art and Depression* (Minneapolis: University of

Minnesota Press, 2006), p. xix;
Dominic Fox, *Cold World: The Aesthetics
of Dejection and the Politics of Militant
Dysphoria* (Winchester, Hants.:
Zero Books, 2009), p. 6.

**24** Sigmund Freud, *The Interpretation of
Dreams*, *Penguin Freud Library*, vol. IV
(Harmondsworth: Penguin, 1980),
pp. 671–2, 705. See also Robert J. C.
Young's essay, 'Freud's Secret:
*The Interpretation of Dreams* Was a
Gothic Novel'. Available at: <http://
robertjcyoung.com/Freudssecret.pdf>.

**25** Mark 5: 2, 9.

**26** James Naremore, *On Kubrick* (London:
BFI, 2007), p. 203.

**27** Patrick McGilligan, *Jack's Life:
A Biography of Jack Nicholson* (London:
Hutchinson, 1994), p. 312.

**28** Alex Ross, *The Rest Is Noise:
Listening to the Twentieth Century*
(London: Fourth Estate, 2012),
pp. 510, 484.

**29** Paul Griffiths, *György Ligeti* (London:
Robson, 1983), p. 34.

**30** Mayersberg, 'Overlook Hotel', p. 258.

**31** For discussion of the Magical Negro,
see Christopher John Farley, 'That Old
Black Magic', *Time Magazine*
(27 November 2000); Susan Gonzalez,
'Director Spike Lee Slams "Same Old"
Black Stereotypes in Today's Films', *Yale
Bulletin* (2 March 2001); and Nnedi
Okorafor-Mbachu, 'Stephen King's
Super-Duper Magical Negroes', *Strange
Horizons* (25 October 2004). All of these
are available online. For a fuller survey,
see Matthew W. Hughey, 'Cinethetic
Racism: White Redemption and Black
Stereotypes in "Magical Negro" Films',
*Social Problems*, vol. 56 no. 3 (August
2009), pp. 543–77.

**32** Ciment, *Kubrick*, p. 192.

**33** Thomson, *Overexposures*, p. 327.

**34** Kael, 'Devolution', p. 4.

**35** Ovid, *Metamorphosis*, trans.
A. Melville (Oxford: Oxford University
Press, 1986), Book 8, pp. 175–6.

**36** Michel Foucault, *Death and the
Labyrinth: The World of Raymond Roussel*
(London: Athlone, 1986), p. 87.

**37** Robert Kolker, *A Cinema of Loneliness:
Penn, Stone, Kubrick, Scorsese, Spielberg and
Altman*, 3rd edn. (Oxford: Oxford
University Press, 2000), p. 106.

**38** See Georges Bataille, 'The Labyrinth'
(1930), reprinted in full online at:
<http://www.angelfire.com/nv/
readpiss/Labyrinth.txt>.

**39** Georg Lukács, Preface to his
*Theory of the Novel*, reprinted in full
at: <http://www.marxists.org/archive/
lukacs/works/theory-novel/
preface.htm>.

**40** Friedrich Nietzsche, extract from
*A Nietzsche Reader*, selected and
translated by R. J. Hollingdale (London:
Penguin, 1977), p. 249.

# Credits

**The Shining**
USA/1980

**Directed by**
Stanley Kubrick
**Produced by**
Stanley Kubrick
**Executive Producer**
Jan Harlan
**Screenplay by**
Stanley Kubrick and
Diane Johnson, based
on the novel by
Stephen King
**Director of Photography**
John Alcott

© 1980. Warner Bros.
**Production Companies**
Warner Bros., Hawk
Films, Peregrine
Productions, Producer
Circle Company
**Studio**
EMI-Elstree

**2nd Unit Photographer**
Douglas Milsome
**2nd Unit Photography**
MacGillivray-Freeman
Films
**Steadicam Operator**
Garrett Brown
**Camera Operators**
Kelvin Pike
James Devis
**Special Effects**
Alan Whibley
Les Hillman
Dick Parker

**Edited by**
Ray Lovejoy
**Assistant Editors**
Gill Smith
Gordon Stainforth
**Production Designer**
Roy Walker
**Art Director**
Les Tomkins
**Make-up**
Tom Smith
**Wardrobe Supervisors**
Ken Lawton
Ron Beck
**Sound Recording**
Ivan Sharrock
Richard Daniel
**Sound Editors**
Wyn Ryder
Dino di Campo
Jack Knight
**Music**
Wendy Carlos and Rachel
Elkind, 'The Shining';
Carlos, 'Rocky
Mountains'; Carlos,
'Shining/Heartbeat';
György Ligeti, *Lontano*;
Béla Bartók, *Music for
Strings, Percussion and
Celesta*; Krzysztof
Penderecki, *Polymorphia*;
Penderecki, *De Natura
Sonoris No. 1* and *No. 2*;
Penderecki, *Utrenja II:
Evangelia* and *Kanon
Paschy*; Penderecki, *Kanon
for Orchestra and Tape*;
Penderecki, *The
Awakening of Jacob*; Jack
Hylton and His

Orchestra, 'Masquerade';
Ray Noble and His
Orchestra, 'Midnight, the
Stars and You' and 'It's
All Forgotten Now'; Henry
Hall and the Gleneagles
Hotel Band, 'Home'.

**CAST**
**Jack Nicholson**
Jack Torrance
**Shelley Duvall**
Wendy Torrance
**Danny Lloyd**
Danny Torrance
**Scatman Crothers**
Dick Hallorann
**Barry Nelson**
Stuart Ullmann
**Philip Stone**
Delbert Grady
**Joe Turkel**
Lloyd the barman
**Anne Jackson**
doctor
**Tony Burton**
Larry Durkin
**Lia Beldam**
young woman in bath
**Billie Gibson**
old woman in bath
**Barry Dennen**
Bill Watson
**David Baxt**
first forest ranger
**Manning Redwood**
second forest ranger
**Lisa and Louise Burns**
Grady's daughters
**Robin Pappas**
nurse

**Alison Coleridge**
Susie
**Burnell Tucker**
policeman
**Jana Sheldon**
stewardess
**Kate Phelps**
receptionist
**Norman Gay**
injured guest

Premiered in New York
on 23 May 1980.
Running time:
144 minutes.
Premiered in London on
3 October 1980.
Running time:
119 minutes.

# Bibliography

Alcott, John, 'Photographing Stanley
    Kubrick's *The Shining*', *American
    Cinematographer*, vol. 61 no. 8
    (August 1980), pp. 780–8.
Bettelheim, Bruno, *The Uses of
    Enchantment: The Meaning and
    Importance of Fairy Tales* (London:
    Penguin, 1991).
Bingham, Dennis, 'The Displaced
    Auteur: A Reception History of *The
    Shining*', in Falsetto (ed.), *Perspectives
    on Stanley Kubrick*, pp. 284–306.
Brophy, Philip, 'Horrality: The Textuality
    of Contemporary Horror Films',
    *Screen*, vol. 27 no. 1 (January–
    February 1986), pp. 2–13.
Brown, Garrett, 'The Steadicam and
    *The Shining*', in Falsetto (ed.),
    *Perspectives on Stanley Kubrick*,
    pp. 273–83.
Ciment, Michel, *Kubrick* (London:
    Collins, 1983).
Cocks, Geoffrey, 'Death by Typewriter:
    Stanley Kubrick, the Holocaust and
    *The Shining*', in Cocks *et al.* (eds),
    *Depth of Field*, pp. 185–217.
———, James Diedrick and Glenn
    Perusek (eds), *Depth of Field: Stanley
    Kubrick, Film, and the Uses of History*
    (Madison: University of Wisconsin
    Press, 2006).
Combs, Richard, '*The Shining*', *Monthly
    Film Bulletin*, vol. 47 no. 562
    (November 1980), pp. 221–2.
Cooper, David, *The Death of the Family*
    (Harmondsworth: Penguin, 1971).
Crilly, Ciaran, 'The Bigger Picture:
    Ligeti's Music and the Films of
    Stanley Kubrick', in Louise
    Duschesneau and Wolfgang Marx
    (eds), *György Ligeti: Of Foreign Lands

    and Strange Sounds* (Woodbridge,
    Suffolk: Boydell Press, 2011),
    pp. 245–54.
Curtis, Barry, *Dark Places: The Haunted
    House in Film* (London: Reaktion, 2008).
Egan, Kate, *The Evil Dead* (London:
    Wallflower Press, 2011).
Falsetto, Mario (ed.), *Perspectives
    on Stanley Kubrick* (New York:
    G. K. Hall, 1996).
Fiedler, Leslie, *Love and Death in the
    American Novel* (Champaign, IL:
    Dalkey Archive, 1998).
Fox, Dominic, *Cold World: The Aesthetics
    of Dejection and the Politics of Militant
    Dysphoria* (Winchester, Hants.:
    Zero Books, 2009).
Freud, Sigmund, 'Family Romances'
    (1909), in *Standard Edition of the
    Complete Psychological Works*, vol. IX
    (London: Hogarth Press, 1959),
    pp. 235–42.
———, *The Interpretation of Dreams*,
    *Penguin Freud Library*, vol. IV
    (Harmondsworth: Penguin, 1980).
———, 'From the History of an Infantile
    Neurosis: The "Wolf Man"' (1918), in
    *Case Histories II*, *Penguin Freud Library*,
    vol. IX (Harmondsworth: Penguin,
    1981), pp. 227–366.
———, 'The "Uncanny"' (1919), in *Art
    and Literature*, *Penguin Freud Library*,
    vol. XIV (Harmondsworth: Penguin,
    1985), pp. 339–76.
Gengaro, Christine Lee, *Listening to Stanley
    Kubrick: The Music in His Films*
    (Lanham, MD: Scarecrow Press, 2013).
Geuens, Jean-Pierre, 'Visuality and
    Power: The Work of the Steadicam',
    *Film Quarterly*, vol. 47 no. 2 (Winter
    1993–4), pp. 8–17.

Goodrich-Freer, Ada and John, Marquess of Bute, *The Alleged Haunting of Ballechin House* (London: Redway, 1899).

Griffiths, Paul, *György Ligeti* (London: Robson, 1983).

Hawkins, Joan, *Cutting Edge: Art-Horror and the Horrific Avant-Garde* (Minneapolis: University of Minnesota Press, 2000).

Kael, Pauline, 'Devolution', in *Taking It All In* (London: Marion Boyars, 1986), pp. 1–7.

Keeler, Greg, '*The Shining*: Ted Kramer Has a Nightmare', *Journal of Popular Film and Television*, vol. 8 no. 4 (Winter 1981), pp. 2–8.

Kolker, Robert, *A Cinema of Loneliness: Penn, Stone, Kubrick, Scorsese, Spielberg and Altman*, 3rd edn. (Oxford: Oxford University Press, 2000).

Krohn, Bill, *Stanley Kubrick* (Paris: Cahiers du Cinéma, 2007).

Jameson, Fredric, 'Historicism in *The Shining*', in *Signatures of the Visible* (London: Routledge, 1992), pp. 112–34.

Johnson, Diane, 'Writing *The Shining*', in Cocks et al., *Depth of Field*, pp. 55–61.

King, Stephen, *The Shining* (London: New English Library, 1977).

———, *Danse Macabre* (London: Hodder, 1981).

Lightman, Herb, 'Photographing Stanley Kubrick's *The Shining*: An Interview with John Alcott', in Falsetto (ed.), *Perspectives on Stanley Kubrick*, pp. 260–72.

LoBrutto, Vincent, *Stanley Kubrick* (London: Faber, 1997).

Lovecraft, H. P., *Supernatural Horror in Literature* (New York: Dover, 1973).

Luckhurst, Roger, *The Invention of Telepathy, 1870–1901* (Oxford: Oxford University Press, 2002).

McCaffery, Larry, 'Talking about "The Shining" with Diane Johnson', *Chicago Review*, vol. 33 no. 1 (Summer 1981), pp. 75–9.

McGilligan, Patrick, *Jack's Life: A Biography of Jack Nicholson* (London: Hutchinson, 1994).

Mayersberg, Paul, 'The Overlook Hotel', in Falsetto (ed.), *Perspectives on Stanley Kubrick*, pp. 253–9.

Mintz, Steven, *Huck's Raft: A History of Childhood in America* (Cambridge, MA: Harvard University Press, 2004).

Naremore, James, *On Kubrick* (London: BFI, 2007).

Nelson, Thomas Allen, *Kubrick: Inside a Film Artist's Maze* (Bloomington: Indiana University Press, 1982).

Newman, Kim, *Nightmare Movies: Horror on the Screen since the 1960s* (London: Bloomsbury, 2011).

Nowell, Richard, *Blood Money: A History of the First Teen Slasher Film Cycle* (London: Continuum, 2011).

Paul, William, *Laughing, Screaming: Modern Hollywood Horror and Comedy* (New York: Columbia University Press, 1994).

Phillips, Gene D. and Rodney King (eds), *The Encyclopedia of Stanley Kubrick* (New York: Facts on File, 2006).

Pudovkin, V. I., *Film Technique and Film Acting*, ed. Ivor Montague (London: Vision, 1968).

Robinson, David, 'Sad Mystery of Kubrick's Latest', *The Times*, 3 October 1980.

Romney, Jonathan, 'Resident Phantoms', *Sight & Sound* (September 1999), pp. 8–11.

Ross, Alex, *The Rest Is Noise: Listening to the Twentieth Century* (London: Fourth Estate, 2012).

Ross, Christine, *The Aesthetics of Disengagement: Contemporary Art and Depression* (Minneapolis: University of Minnesota Press, 2006).

Thomson, David, *Overexposures: The Crisis in American Filmmaking* (New York: Morrow, 1981).

Titterington, P. L., 'Kubrick and *The Shining*', *Sight & Sound* (February 1981), pp. 117–21.

Tudor, Andrew, *Monsters and Mad Scientists: A Cultural History of the Horror Movie* (Oxford: Blackwell, 1989).

Walker, Alexander, *Stanley Kubrick, Director*, revised edn. (New York: Norton, 1999).

Wood, Robin, *Hollywood from Vietnam to Reagan* (New York: Columbia University Press, 1986).

# Don't miss out! Sign up to our mailing list to receive news about BFI Film and TV Classics and win a free bundle of books worth £100!

Each book in the BFI Film and TV Classics series honours a landmark of world cinema and television.

With new titles publishing every year, the series represent some of the best writing on film and TV available in print today.

In order to enter, first sign up via:
http://www.palgrave.com/resources/mailing.asp
and then simply email bfi@palgrave.com with your
name, email address and NEW BFI CONTACT in the
subject header.

Entry offer ends: 03/01/14. The winner will be
contacted via email by 31/01/14.